13 QUESTIONS FOR THE NEXT ECONOMY

Susan Briante

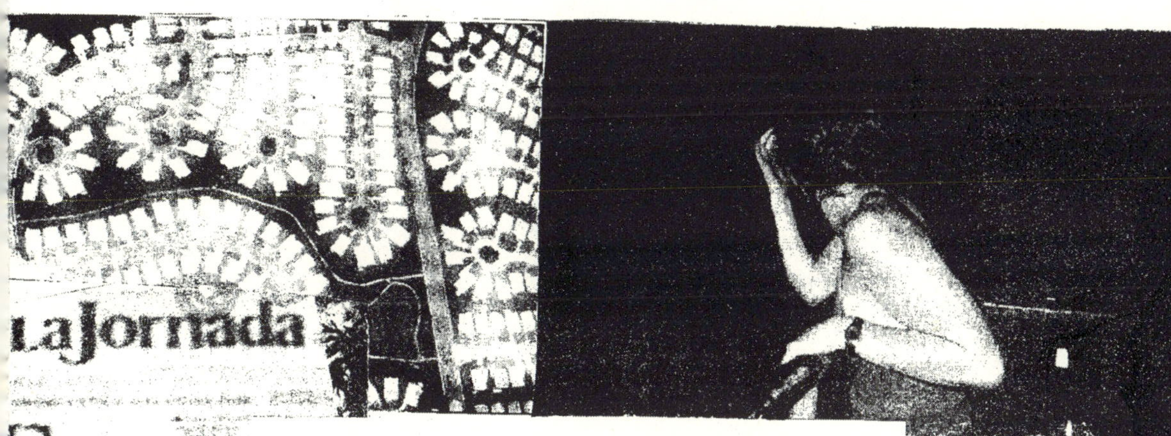

new and selected works

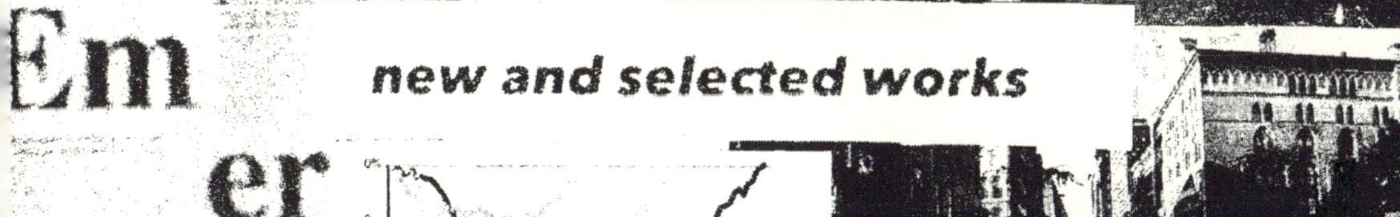

Published by Noemi Press, Inc. A Nonprofit Literary organization. www.noemipress.org.

Cover & Book Design by Roda Avelar
Typeset in Avenir Next Condensed, Eskorte Latin, & Mrs Eaves OT

ISBN: 978-1-955992-66-4

13 QUESTIONS FOR THE NEXT ECONOMY

Susan Briante

new and selected works

(Fotografía de frente)
(Huella digital del pulgar derecho)
DATOS DEL TITULA
Nombre: SUSAN CAROL BRIANTE M
Nacionalidad: NORTEAMERICANA
e-board garden a
ie freeway loops a
scount merchand
ohobia-induc
OCCUPY WALL S

This book is a spreadsheet, is a check registry, a series of monthly statements that span decades, is an aesthetic arrangement of notes culled from (one) life under late capitalism in the late 20th and early 21st centuries. It exists because the press that published my first three collections of poetry went out of business.

This book is about money!

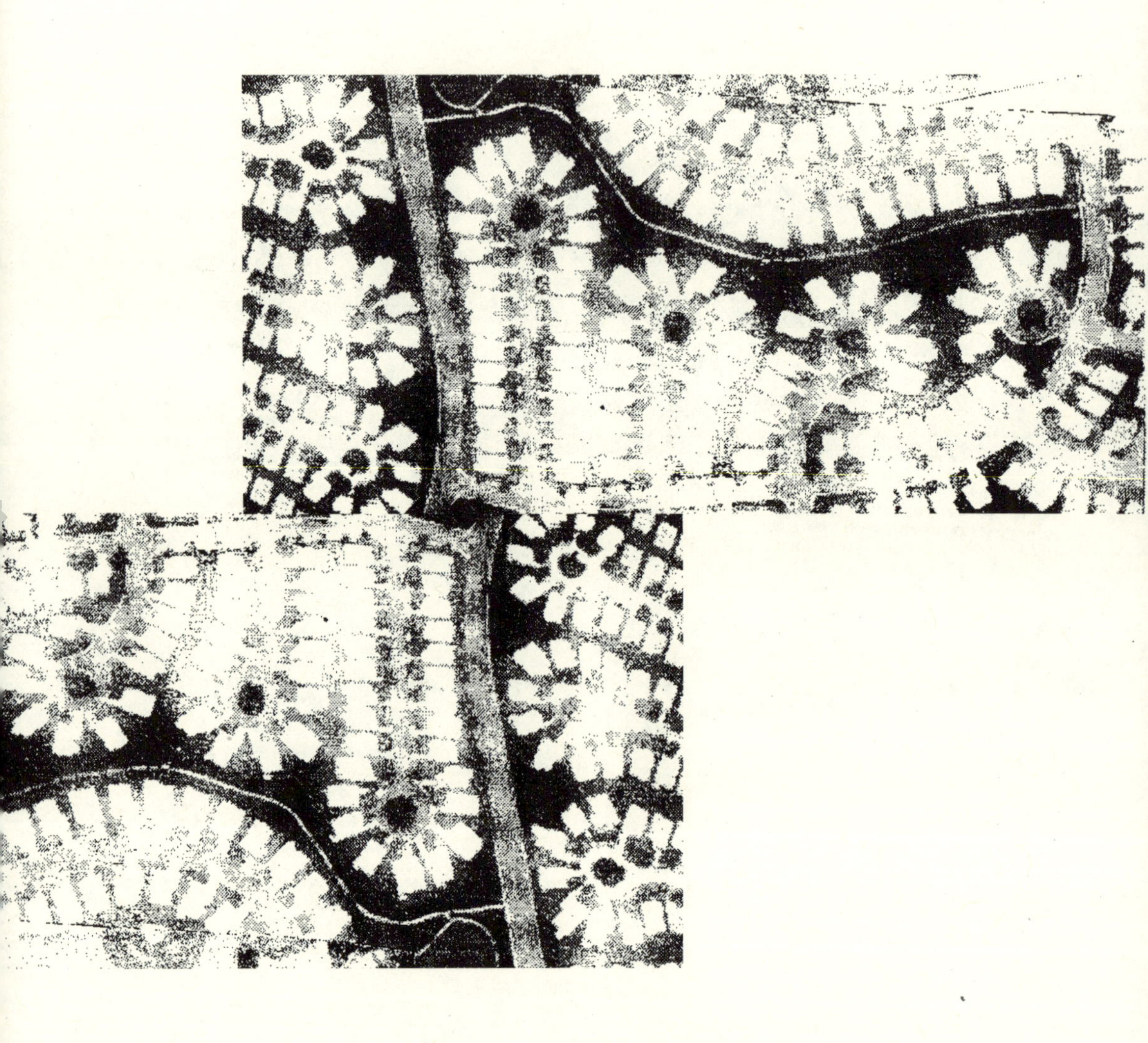

13 QUESTIONS FOR THE NEXT ECONOMY

On the side of the road, white cardboard in the shape of a man,
          illegible script. A signpost with scrawl: *Will pay cash for diabetes strips.*

A system under the system with its black box.   *Disability hearing?*
a billboard reads. *Trouble with Social Security?* Where does the riot begin?

Spark of dry grass, Russian thistle in flames, or butterflies bobbing
as if pulled by unseen strings   through the alleyway.

My mother's riot would have been peace. A bicycle wheel
chained to a concrete planter. What metaphor

can I use to describe the children sleeping in cages in detention
centers? Birds pushed fenceward by a breeze? A train of brake lights

extending? Mesquite pods mill under our feet
on a rainless sidewalk. What revolution   will my daughter feed?

A break-the-state, twig-quick snap or a long divining   as if
for water? A cotton silence? A death?   Who will read this

in the next economy, the one that comes after the one that kills us?
What lessons will we take from the side of the road? A wooden crucifix,

a white bicycle, a pinwheel, a poem
waiting to be redacted: What would you cross out?

TABLE OF CONTENTS

NEW WORK

MY REVOLUTION

my revolution eats arsenic/ chews lead grapes/ makes handprints in cheap green paint/ makes spit bubbles pulls off her diaper/ negates/ my revolution tells me to stop singing/ starts screaming/ calls for me and kicks and bites/ my revolution wakes

in the middle of the night/ cold in her piss twist tied by blankets/ we offered in love/ in resistance/ my revolution would kill us in the middle of the night/ when she cannot legitimize/ when she shreds vocabulary/ mythology/ when she will not tolerate our singing/ my lullaby/ my revolution

does not recognize me/ explores new syntax/ names her parts/ shames me/ because of my shame of mine/ demands I name everyone in the house

my revolution spits out cereal/ spits out arsenic/ implicates me with spit

my revolution refuses to believe she will be cured by honey or vinegar or elderberry/ has no faith that we can get off the grid/ has no currency but hunger and need and her eyes (O the eyes of my revolution and their fuckery)/ my revolution burns

like a city under siege/ tears like a rocket through the cold swirl of galaxy/ through the cold calculation of capital/ my revolution sets flame to every prison caged inside me

TO ERASURES, ERASURES

1.

Salt in the mouth, multitudes of mouth in the Palo Verde trees, buzzing emergency circulating poisonous flags and their flowering green,

fig beetle with armor the color of currencies, who mouths me sidewise from its middle wings: when you careen across a border, do you exceed or collapse it?

A desert exceeds, a border snares: a snake drawn to river, a river to erasures, erasures of footprints and flag, seasons that exceed, the poisonous expatriate green

beetle like a font, like a script, like

thoughts in a sky
to awaken us to our discomfort and the sky.

2.

The fig beetle fights for sap, fights for fleshiest fruit, that's capitalism, font in its teeth, everything that dies after it feeds: the document of its hunger.

Roots under, under

the Palo Verde trees kind of talking. Maybe that's capitalism, too. The roots. Maybe that's the nation spreading

or the sprawl of law, hysterical as history, grammar wobbles underfoot, sand shifts like a sky, law touches unpredictably as a breeze, documents from which we nibbled away a little shade.

All the while, the sun: a federal agent scanning us.

3.

Thought moves across you weightless as currency
clouds across a Sonoran sky

inscribing a promise, a season
completing a circuit of labor and capital

or this sentence: *I am ashamed to be an American.*

How does it end? Like cloud? Can you finger its border at my lips? On the page? In the cool of your ear? Does it canyon or arroyo inside you?

4.

Around the town square, old men rev motorcycles, buzz. Black helmet chrome armor, beetled out at the 4th of July parade, pure plume and fragile as a tongue. Mouth me, full throttle sun. Flags on the antennae of pickup trucks trembling like bugs.

Every community swings a door.

A nation scrawls on a page of landscape, a document flawed, but with a pronoun just loose enough to make a little cave, to stage a little nest; a document to cast just a sliver of shade under clouds thinned and ruled without margins.

5.

I am ashamed to be an American.
I am afraid to be an American.
I am working to be an American.
I am walking miles across the desert to be ________.

6.

Severed said the Palo Verde tree and threw down a line of shade, black boxed. A beetle pulses through the docu-sky,

a poem chattering on, a mouthful of wings, poems chattering to themselves about the deaths and the heat, limbs twitching.

7.

Hum in the mouth of currencies, spit in the mouth of state, to make a fist of words, to mourn in the mouth, the beetle flies illegible, unaccountable, to song out the throat with no visa, no work permit.

Not even the sky is equal access. Make the page roof, suture the mouth in penance. We walk alone in the text

as a wordless cloud drifts past like a citizen, miles away

and touches no one, saves no one.

OLEANDERS SHRINK UNDER PRECISELY THIS

Oleanders shrink under precisely this
sun, and A-10s make coming home
circles in a sky bristling at their touch
I try to imagine storm cloud, brushfire,
meadow, just enough
space for my family and me
to live without injuring any possible *you*
but all I can hear is airstrip as the A-10s
trace their cursive script and the prickly pear
blossoms this far into drought, looking
first like a fist, then a mouth

THE MESSENGERS

The comet looked like a smudge in the sky, hung above the winter parking lot of my parents' northern New Jersey condominium.

Across the country, thirty-nine men and women in black shirts, sweat pants, and Nike shoes took phenobarbital mixed with applesauce, drank vodka and secured plastic bags over their heads, waiting for transport, trying to intersect with a trajectory inscribed light years above them.

Despite the fact that it sped along at nearly 100,000 mph with respect to the solar system, from the parking lot of my parents' northern New Jersey condominium, Hale-Bopp did not appear to be moving.

*

In the first dream about my mother after her death, her eyes appeared glazed and still. She said nothing. Her friend, Marie, handed me a set of car keys, so I could take my mother somewhere. As soon as I felt the keys in my hand, my mother disappeared.

In the second dream, a small iridescent blue snake coiled in dirt. Black bands circled its body, a translucent skin twisted beside it. As it burrowed into the ground, I knew it was my mother.

To dream a blue snake stands for religiosity. When a snake sheds skin, the dreamer outgrows herself, leaves behind old existence and personality.

Later I found an image on the internet that confirmed the snake was poisonous, a blue krait.

*

In grade school, I saw constellations in the lead black circles of my answers on standardized tests and hoped beyond academic assessment these penciled constellations (here a man, there a flower) would reveal something remarkable about me—and someone would notice.

*

I had a ______ childhood.
I had a childhood.
There was a childhood.

*

A diagram in my acupuncturist's office indicates pressure points for auricular therapy. In the image, a skeleton is superimposed on a representation of the ear to indicate correspondence between points on a lobe and locations on the body,

like images of nautilus shells superimposed on photographs of spiral galaxies.

*

To the ancients, comets brought messages from heaven foretelling of war, crop failure, plague, and other disasters. Some saw the comet as a woman's head with long flowing hair; others thought the comet appeared to be a fiery sword. In ancient Rome, the Emperor Nero believed a comet's arrival predicted his assassination—and he called for the death of every one of his successors.

Solidifying balls of rock, dust, water, ice, and frozen gases such as carbon dioxide, carbon monoxide, methane, and ammonia, comets form from materials released during the creation and destruction of stars.

Some scientists believe comets bombarding a young Earth may have brought water to our planet. Some scientists believe many of the components of DNA and RNA, the building blocks of life, may have formed on comets.

*

In some acupuncture diagrams, it is not a skeleton superimposed on the ear but a coiled fetus: its head hung toward the lobe, feet curled in the swirls of the ear canal. In other images, it is a mother bent to shelter an infant.

*

"Do you want me to poison you?" my mother screamed, shaking a container of salt at me across the kitchen table. I was probably four or five. I wanted to help her cook something. I don't remember why her anger uncoiled.

*

In winter, I look for Orion and the "W" of Cassiopeia, hunter and queen,
compass points slowly turning against a backdrop of sky.

I have a friend who says she doesn't believe in constellations.
She just sees flecks of light,
says you can make any picture you want.

*

My parents married when they were 19. Until then, my mother lived with her father (an abusive alcoholic), her mother, a brother and two sisters.

In July 1967, five months before my birth, my mother was 29 years old. She had two sons (seven and nine). Her hometown of Newark was rioting. And my father was probably cheating on her.

Your mother is a survivor, a therapist once told me. And you are, too.

*

maps laid upon maps then crumpled in a fist

until they create alternate topographies

*

My acupuncturist places a needle between my forefinger and thumb. I grimace. What at first feels like a pinprick below my left pinky toe blossoms into a pain so deep, tears well in my eyes.

From the perspective of ancient Chinese medicine, energy (chi) moves through the body like electricity on a grid. When energy floods one area or becomes blocked in another, illness—a black out, a power surge—occurs.

My acupuncturist never leaves a painful needle in place as pain evidences a necessary shift in energy.

*

In another dream, I hold pink wrapping paper that covered a book my mother had given my father for their anniversary. I cannot remember the book's title or seeing my parents in the dream, just the wrapping paper—a rigid, emptied cocoon.

In another dream, I steal gifts intended for other women, pulling manila envelopes out of mailboxes. I apologize, saying: I am crazy with grief from my mother's death.

In another, the sky looks like crumpled paper pinpricked with lights.

And when I wake in a ruffle of brainwave and tatter of morning,
where is my mother?

*

Common methods for communicating with the dead include:

- shifting focus to sharpen the sixth sense
- attempting to talk through the power of the mind
- mirror gazing
- listening for Electronic Voice Phenomenon
- looking for variations in Electromagnetic Pulses
- prayer
- contacting a medium
- asking the deceased to answer yes or no questions by responding with a series of knocks or by "gently pushing a power button on a flashlight to give an answer"

*

When I was a child, I read all the books about the major constellations in my elementary school library—then all the books on the Greek myths associated with them.

Sometimes Cassiopeia sits upon her throne. Sometimes she hangs from the sky chained to a chair. Sometimes she holds her mirror.

Where Western astronomers see Cassiopeia, the Chinese see "the great chariot." In Arab atlases,

Cassiopeia's stars form part of "the tinted hand" either a woman's hand painted with henna or the bloodied hand of Muhammad's daughter Fatima.

*

Chinese physicians know the space between cells
to be as important as the cells themselves.

*

My dreams about Craig started even before he was presumed dead, in the first days he went missing on a hike in Japan. When he appeared in my dreams, he talked very directly about our relationship and what it meant to him. In one of the dreams, we sat in a parked school bus with our arms around each other.

In one of the last dreams, he lay face up as if on a stretcher, gauze covering his mouth, his eyes closed.

I asked him to stay.

I heard his voice although his bandaged mouth did not move.

And he told me he had to go.

*

Heaven's Gate cult members believed they needed to abandon the vehicles of their bodies in order to reach a higher level of existence. They believed a UFO hid in Hale-Bopp's tail waiting to transport them. Authorities found cult members in their beds in a rented San Diego mansion, heads and torsos covered by a square purple cloth.

In a video taped days before the mass suicide, a cult leader explained: "It was the only way to evacuate earth."

*

My sister-in-law calls me crying. My mother had just phoned to tell her she was such a good daughter-in-law and wife and mother. My sister-in-law worried my mother was saying good-bye.

My mother called me in the middle of that conversation. When we spoke, she said nothing out of the ordinary. We talked about my daughter. We talked about my mother's symptoms. By that time, you could feel a hardened tumor on her liver. Pain radiated down her neck, shoulder and right side.

My mother and I talked every day, sometimes twice a day, until she entered hospice. When she did, I flew home to see her. When I arrived, she said nothing to acknowledge me. Staring straight ahead at photographs of her grandchildren, she asked: "Who are they?"

The next day when I told her I loved her, she said: "Thank you." That was the last day she spoke.

*

The European Space Agency's Rosetta spacecraft, named for the stone that helped unlock the language of Egyptian hieroglyphs, traveled for 10 years through our solar system to rendezvous with comet CG 67P. After hovering in its orbit for a little more than three months, Rosetta sent down the lander, Philae, to the comet's surface, a feat never before achieved, on November 12, 2014, just weeks after my mother's death.

*

A final post on the Heaven's Gate website declares: "Whether Hale-Bopp has a 'companion' (UFO) or not is irrelevant from our perspective...Hale-Bopp's approach is the 'marker' we've been waiting for..."

*

Whatever we might believe about UFOs or the afterlife, we know very little about what cult members experienced after they lay down in their beds in their rented San Diego mansion for the last time in March 1997.

Researchers report a brief but significant spike in brain activity lasting for 30 to 180 seconds at or near the time of death, despite a preceding drop in brain activity.

Another study found an increase in brain activity of rats in the 30-second period after the animals' hearts stopped beating.

*

We don't need a scientific study to feel how death reroutes the neurological pathways of survivors, coding and recoding, carving a little moat around every memory of our dead

and every time we contact their absence

a little spark
a searing jolt.

*

A photo of me dressed in my doctoral regalia sat wedged in the corner of the mirror above my mother's dresser. She placed no other photos there except a mass card with the image of Jesus.

*

Look up to see a hand tinted with blood or painted with henna.
Look again, a queen slides from her throne.

*

Psychologist, Allen Botkin has developed a method he calls Inducing Communication After Death (ICAD) to help patients with Post-Traumatic Stress Disorder (PTSD) and those struggling with grief.

One patient treated using ICAD reports having spoken to her deceased father and his twin as well as being visited by her three most beloved dogs. Another patient, a Vietnam War veteran, reports having received a hug from a Vietnamese child killed in the war.

Botkin's technique derives from a treatment of PTSD known as Eye-Movement Desensitization and Reprocessing (EMDR). The treatment allows patients to process traumatic experiences more quickly than they would through talk therapy. In EMDR, as well as Botkin's ICAD, the guided rapid back and forth movement of the patient's eyes (mimicking the rapid eye movements of sleep) put the brain into what has been described as "a higher processing mode associated with dreams."

*

My daughter and I lie in her bed listening to an audio story about a caterpillar who wishes to travel to a neighboring stalk of milkweed. The caterpillar asks his brother about the stalk. No one who has tried to get there, his brother tells him, has ever returned. Nonetheless, the caterpillar decides he will attempt the journey. He eats well. He grows fat. And on the day before he plans to set out for the milkweed, he becomes very tired and falls into a deep sleep.

He dreams in flashes of orange and black.

When he wakes, he unfurls a pair of orange and black wings and flies to the neighboring milkweed.

*

Among several possible interpretations, the caterpillar's tale strikes me as a metaphor for the difficulty of communicating across our transformations.

*

Astronomers continue to track Hale-Bopp, detecting it in December 2010 at 30.7 astronomical units away from the sun, again, in August 2012 at a distance of 33.2 AU, and most recently in 2022 when it was 46.2 AU from the sun despite previous concerns that it would be no longer observable when it became difficult to distinguish from the many distant galaxies of similar brightness.

*

In my acupuncturist's office, I stare up at acoustic tiles set in gold frames, certain that while I have rested in this position for hours during my appointments there are still new patterns to be perceived.

"Are you feeling run down?" my acupuncturist asks as she takes my pulse.

Yes.

After she sets the needles and leaves the room, my mind bends from daydream to sleep. I feel my body float half submerged in water, my face rising just above its surface. In dream, I see a red, yellow, and blue striped staff stirring a liquid. I don't know whose hand guides it.

*

In a dream I stand on a city sidewalk with my college boyfriend. My mother should be here, I tell him.

So I wait for her.

*

4.9 % of the universe is atomic matter
26.6% of the universe is mysterious dark matter
68.5% of the universe is dark energy

*

I save voicemails from my mother on my phone. In the last one, she reports that she is coming home from the hospital. She says she wants to get some Sprite because she has heartburn. She calls me honey. She tells me she loves me.

*

Not the end of ______ but the end of the moment when ______.

*

In August 2014, Rosetta became the first spacecraft to orbit a comet. In November of that same year, Philae landed on the surface and began sending photographs and readings back to earth for 57 hours before its battery ran out.

The mission ended with Rosetta's controlled impact on the comet's surface in 2016.
Scientists continue to sift through data sent from Rosetta and Philae, searching for information about the origins of Earth and our solar system

coded in icy dust and particle spark,
hidden in a smudge that looks fixed against the sky,
a fingerprint on a cold window of night.

WHAT COMES AFTER US

I stalled at the stoplight, imagined old rivers raging.
The quarry contracted. Not much more to carry.

My father sped ahead, in the back
of a white medical van strapped

in his hospital gown, his headlights
scalpeling through snow, a thin blanket

across his lap in the cold. No light
from the west, but a glow from the hospital garage.

And my car could not follow him.
        Tonight the Geminids radiate from Castor

in the east, trees bare except for seed pod. We can't know
what comes after us. I can't pray to my father's god.

Pray for my father, pray for the dead
leaves clinging to the sycamore. I am trying

to sit with death, receipts rustling at the roots
of a parking lot tree.   After we go, will it have been enough

to have recorded the ember-teal of dawn? The juiced up
autumn leaves? Enough to hear wrens

flick their notes to the breeze, my father's complaints
on the phone. Enough to promise to come home

while I stayed away, while a dark sky curved above me?
There's a poem that would say *YES*   but I can't write it.

Fuck the medical van slurring through the suburban dusk
four months before my father's death,

highway gnawing my hometown's edge, afternoons
staggering to bed.   We can't know what comes for us.

Fuck the care coordinator, the nursing home's shitty care,
my father's medical debts. Fuck the hospital's thin blanket,

the parking garage lights stealing sunset.

Details from WHAT COMES AFTER US

The nurses slid pills into your shallow palm,
the cure factory shuffled you through its stations

learning to walk again, refusing to eat. You rioted against the doctors. Your discomfort
became a harvest, until you were no longer my father

a smile or worse or less
the last thing you said

penciled calculations
sometimes a spreadsheet is an elegy

a story I tell:
a tube placed between your teeth
all for one more breath

for weeks I wanted to lift you from the shell of your voice, your tremble
with my small machines of speech,

inadequate as a government check

a billing clerk to document your transformation

es Dad's biggest problem is depression,
think there's something else going on. She
rine culture on him. They will have the
y will probably not have the urine culture
UTI that could account for his loss of
of taste, she said that could be caused by
on list tomorrow.

Westgate Condo Fee	$	340.00	Cash Withd
Healthcare 1	$	236.00	Supermark
Healthcare 2	$	87.00	Gasoline
Etown Gas			
PSE&G			
NJ American Water			
R/E Taxes ($2,042 / 3)			
Auto Insurance ($1,517 / 12)			
Life Insurance			
Home Owners Insurance ($822 / 12)			

I talked to the head n
which I am not sure I
said they are doing a
results of the first two
results until Monday.
appetite, dizziness, etc
medication. She said s

A SERIES OF PULSES

The sky puckers at this hour.
Crickets trill, harmonize, syncopate,

and that looks like cottonwood
and that looks like sugar maple.

I could lean against the window, clean off my glasses,
name something, save something.

Debt shock, price shocks, currency shocks,
shock of leaves on this leaftlit morning.

There's nothing to describe. Describe
the moss between the shingles,

warm and southerly brick face, vaulted branches,
brush where the forest finds its edge.

The abandoned torture center under the shopping mall
in Buenos Aires makes its own ugly metaphor.

The first notes of a train whistle like scales,
and when I hear the first scales, I doubt them.

*

I am asking for numbers that do not exist.

The threat of rain from another horizon rumbles
in your gut.

After the photographs,
we were all writing about hoods and cigarettes, the ball gag,

now it's back to our pregnancies and elms,
your face in a blank window night after night,
a freshly poured foundation,
that's your memory fading, sun screaming
over your body,
a current of branches,
    yes and *yes*.

ALL SWAN WE ARE

Texas rangers explode in lilac the color of nothing in my house. Mesquite trees bleed. A plea for rain, an insult thrown down the wash where a car stalled and a woman drowned yesterday. Some accident,

we are. All swan without flight. All particle, a shuffling engine, running
like quails back and forth across our neighborhood streets. One deviation,

we are. Death maps us like a weather system. One push and the mind thrashes toward form, looks for fingerprints, cause, a red crest on the woodpecker's head. Who knows what grows after.

Show me the place where the dead go, my daughter asks spinning a globe. In our backyard, the Mexican bird of paradise blooms. In the glistening cosmos,

stars go out.

We are nothing. Inside the adobe bricks of our house. Messages make their way through wire. A reading lamp hums on a timer. All night moths rattle from the paradise tree. No need to call it song.

MILKWEED, MIRROR, WINDSHIELD

Today I worked a garden, nothing but weeds until someone named them: Indian blanket, orange milkweed, yerba santa, —

an old story, a sorting

of Johnson from Bermuda grass, pulled up with fingers and tools to make an outdoor classroom, 19 miles from a border where immigration agents sever families as if cutting back vines.

After dinner a pickup idles in a driveway, a fork scrapes a plate, telephone wires vibrate and with each passing car the salt cedar trembles

sunsick in drought, nonnative like most of us.

Claude Monet painted water lilies for decades but waited until the dawn of World War I to paint the eight large panels that curved around me one summer in a Paris museum. Petal and wave, sky and leaf. The signage asked: *Should art act as silvering on a mirror?*

I want art like a shard when the mirror breaks. Under fist or rock hammer.

"Not a mirror up to nature but—"

a collision?

Swallows in the alley continue their conversations. Which calls? Which answers? Art to reminds us families do not vine. The windshield of a pickup can bear the whole sky.

STRIDING, TRACING

To open the body is to turn like Orpheus and lose everything. When working with a 35mm camera, you trust the film advance, feel the long gap between moment and document felt almost nowhere

else now. A child

learns the calendar on a spool of paper. With pictures to mark the day she swims or eats pizza. But only the body registers how the season withdraws from her. Leaf after leaf. This tinned-out autumn light refuses us like mountains at certain elevations or an economic system.

An old woman sits at a table with white sheet draped over her head. In the dream I know she is dead. And I wake to the sound of a street cleaner.

In workshop, I tell my students to "let the seams show." We talk about limits and failure, "productive confusion." In life, I am afraid.

Today the physicists say we might be living in a brane around the event horizon of a collapsed hyper-dimensional star. The physicists say "higher reality," say "soon after the beginning of time."

Every house cradles its dead. In ours, men pull up carpet and asbestos. Fine fibers spindle in the lungs: a persistent melody, a poetics of Monsanto that commodifies the seed.

How do we feed our deaths enough to live proximate—a mirror above the head, a water strider against some surface tension of breath?

To lose the body is to sail like Odysseus, is to wait like Edward Snowden for a country.

Sometimes the dead come to me in dreams. We finish conversations. They hand me objects. Sometimes they have no mouths. Perhaps my mind is a darkroom for some chemical reaction of memory and desire. Perhaps the dead trace their stories on whatever wall they can.

A FORK, A ROCK, A PLASTIC TRAVEL TOOTHBRUSH

death comes anytime
everywhere just today
as my daughter watches a cartoon
about polar bears I read about a man
who watched a bear kill his wife
in the Romanian woods
and the man threw stones
I remember what I cannot picture
how the bear drove the wife's torso
into the ground
an understanding in the half dark
of how "torso" carries the moment
just beyond a stone's throw
when "wife" turned to "corpse"
    will it break?
my daughter asks holding up
a fork, a rock, a plastic travel toothbrush,
a small metal car, a paper plate, a rose bud,
and when I say yes she shakes
her head holds the blossom close
to my face, *but it's not glass*
    we are tuned to shatter
we fear bears, carry stones, a blossom
is luxury for the starving, a cardinal
cries from the tree we cut
back year after year
under which I sit
in red plastic chair
stumble my daughter says
but what she does is fall

WITH A VIEW TO THE BLACK WALNUT TREE

My daughter throws up once or twice a day opening mouth then hands as if to pour out what was clenched. Throws up pillows, backpacks and refrigerators. Builds a version of our cat from pretend vomit, builds a version of our kitchen. I worry

I can't sooth her fears. It is terrible

to witness a body undo itself.

Reading through a pamphlet when my mother entered hospice, I realized I knew as little about death as I once did about birth. Never heard the story of my own, my mother in twilight. When pregnant, I watched video after video my doula showed me: all pant and fluid and scream.

Once in Dallas, I witnessed workmen knock down a wall of our house. With a view to the shivering leaves of our black walnut tree from my seat at the breakfast table, I could not believe how easily inside became out.

It is terrible to wonder how a body undoes itself

to guess what happened to my father after retching in an emergency room. Who came first to help him? What was the last thing he saw? My daughter is terrified of throwing up, panics whenever her stomach aches. What will never be taken from us?

My father died on a hospital gurney with the please-resuscitate order still hanging on his refrigerator. How can I turn away

from his death or my daughter? An order unread. A breath

not taken. There is no consolation just my child's empty hands that she pretends to fill with whatever she imagines roils within.

BLIND CURVE

Took a series of self-portraits on my bed: one hand over my right eye then left as if to mimic another's gaze.

What were you looking for? Farid asks.

On the couch we flip through photographs of male couples (1840–1918). Reading for intimacy: a hand resting mid-thigh, a cheek on a shirt front. Love or sex? The tilt of a chin shows nothing.

A friend learns his lover has HIV. Death is everywhere, he tells me, in his generation. An epidemic breaks, a highball glass slips from a hand at the bar. Some men seek it, he tells me, giving in to a desire

to shift the frame, expose themselves

to a higher power, some turn of star, some splinter of constellation.

My first apartment in Austin perched on a hill at the edge of a blind curve. I'd wake nights to a shattering of headlight, of metal against pavement. The driver squints, freezes: stop light, telephone poll, moon, curb.

The last time I saw my friend, he took our photograph in a parking lot after an opening in the warehouse district. Gaze makes a kind of touch. Death was everywhere that year in all the prize-winning books and Broadway plays.

Once a car skidded into my backyard, another somersaulted through the crosswalk. Once a driver sat on the road smoking a cigarette near his wreck. Once the EMTs pulled a sheet over a body in the street, and the whole night went mute.

Our views multiply as well as what we cannot see. My foot rests against Farid's ankle just out of frame. What moves me. I switch the hand over my eye and room shifts, a slide

drops in a carousel that wheels like a galaxy aching to be seen.

Marbled statues and river views can be found throughout our capital city. Still, it's chaos inside: a concrete and chrome mix of the bureaucratic-brutalism and late-1980s-upper-west-side, packed with roadblocks, vendors, rundown air traffic control towers, protesters, vandals, and open sewers. Unlike our neighbors to the north and south, we no longer produce oil or natural gas. Much of our economic activity is hot, noisy, and overwhelming.

The hurricanes of the 2030s shredded our infrastructure. Aid packages crumbled like the hillsides over our highways. Cars were parked in precisely the same space night after night. By the early 2060s, sources friendly to US interests declared our nation passé. We wore out our carpets. Nobody emptied the ashtrays. For those with enough breath and sail, the ocean awaited. Unfortunately, historical consequence was not a strong national trait.

And yet we continue to believe in our potential to make ourselves great. Remember our grand canyons, our big lakes. Dissolved minerals and microplastics give our tap water the flavor of a people nobly suffering the wounds of civil strife. According to legend, mermaids live in our irrigation canals but can sometimes be seen along the coasts at night. Still, we are not welded to tradition. Imagine a woman slipping a blouse from her shoulders, as she turns to whisper your name. Imagine our nation button by button.

We are fashioning a supercollider from your old mufflers. We have collected change from between our cushions. Our children come versed in a variety of mathematical operations. Now, we have storm drains large enough to swallow a man.

3 de Diciembre del 2015,

Señor Presidente me dirijo a usted haciend

THE VIEW FROM A NATION

r Concederme un Permiso

estar con mis hijos. Tengo 3 hijos que e

y yo me encuentro en Nogales Ro

A border is a cowardice, is a squawking point for politicians.

lobbed over a border fence.

My heart is a stone

Caravans of headlines, headline swarms.
A mob of TV commentators, screaming in our windows.

I did not consent to being a perpetrator.
My labor forged into blade.
My home into a territory, a nation.

Headlines trample fields, stand at the fence in the fields.

A nation erects a border fence to stop a headline,
dismantles a nest to make a line.

A border is a crisis of imagination.

A nation is a parenthesis in the sentence of a life.

The view from a nation is windowless.

Nacieron s hijo. a y quiero
Vivir aq onde su m
le haga na sc eticio Cor f vor
estar co llos, S solo con
favor de nos ur miso estar
poder tr ar ha que a la
edad y tros r Volver a los
puedan seguir su vida solos, por favor conceda-

YOU THE RECOIL

Army transport planes grind through mottled sky, and we wake to news of the beheading.

The recoil will topple you. Study utopia. Look for the settlement. Social dreaming vines: a cul-de-sac above your right eye, a system of discipline and excess

and where river: a story
for a while, and then silence.

A reflection in a tanker car might tempt you toward sympathy. To be coherent. To spindle toward narrative. The events write

us. The news gets swung around by the hair

carelessly, absorbed too quickly. Where a woman died in the arroyo, a sign reads: *Flooding Area.*

ON THE ARCHIVE AND THE UNSEEN

Paper folds make a map or an equation, my daughter asks me to help her make a star with triangles that never close, and learns to print a name

misspelled on or after the 1920 census

what we hoarded or carried or wrinkled on the way

*

As a young woman alone in a strange city, in an economically depressed part of the country, as a journalist for a newspaper that would close, making $13,000 a year, I would drive the outskirts of the midsized, midwestern city

in the evenings: a frontage road, cassette tapes, a 93-cent gallon of gas and packs of American Spirit cigarettes

reading bricks from another economy, archive of our crumbling, at the margins of my employment

I would drive until the highway or the backroad took me to a sign with an unrecognizable name. Turn back (What cloud, what particles and conflicts accumulated behind me?)

to arrive at the school board meeting, in the wake of the teachers' strike, to consult the microfiche at the public library.

How the light tilted or held as I lay on the floor in my bedroom on the night the President first bombed Baghdad.

> In a recurring dream I drive on an unfamiliar road on the outskirts of a city, and when I try to turn the steering wheel, my car flies off a bridge. Sometimes I am alone, sometimes family or friends ride with me. Sometimes I can feel the weightless glee of the car suspended just before impact,

when I hang in the air like a query

*

I practice leaving my phone in another room, I imagine walking into a crowd or boarding a train with no connection to where I am/are going

no way to call you, to tell you I am delayed or okay or lonely

at a place named for its function, aspiration, for what might be seen or done there, for those someone killed to get there.

The documents cross me.

Once I carried recipe cards on which I scribbled to-do lists and phone numbers.

Now we do not know what documents to carry, how the files behind us change our view to the desert around us.

*

My mother became a secretary at an insurance company because no funds were allotted for a girl to go to college in the rations of her working-class family.

In college I worked as an assistant paralegal, learned to log the minutes I summarized, organized, transcribed or photocopied.

We scribbled on legal pads and in manila folders, calculations of fist and forgetfulness

while information, incident, injustice was segregated in thick books, in a hush of who-needs-me, unattached to hyperlink or video feed.

> My mother stopped working when she had her first child at 21 and remained outside the workforce until she became a teacher's aide in her 40s earning $11/hour from the public schools. In a preschool classroom, she constructed records of when a child slept or ate, urinated or defecated: archives of sleep and shit.

*

At home we consult articles with titles like "A 70-Day Web Security Action Plan for Artists and Activists Under Siege." My husband leaves all social media accounts until he returns to them. He uses a secure email server, new text messaging app, a service that scourers the internet for the trafficking of personal information.

I send a scan of my driver's license with my photo and signature blocked out to Intelius group.

I call customer service at MyLife.com.

I wait to receive a text message code from Whitepages.com to confirm the removal of my record.

I follow the instructions on the "Control Your Information" option via the drop-down menu at Radaris.

I am clear in my fear, in the privilege of my Plexiglas terror:

a dream in which a Homeland Security agent stuffs a paperback I ordered from Amazon in 2011 into my mouth.

*

The statistician brings toilet paper rolls to his presentation, stacking them to help students visualize one billion

to know the numbers in their hands.

The mind harbors folds into which pour announcement/information/advertisement/ propaganda/truth/structures of possibility and reaffirmation obscuring what we owe each other

what blanks we are asked to fill.

Do not shrink away.

The texture of my tongue appears in no file (digital or otherwise).

Situate your documents in deep history. Learn to find yourself under the wrong name.

This poem comes to you via Monterrey or the Guangzhou province, from a long branch on a tree of distribution, made to outlive us.

This poem wants to be more than a document of the desert morning: butterfly bush on the easement, fly tapping against a window to feel the meat of its body. And all I cannot see:

bullet at the end of every sentence, drone

at the end of the poem no matter how I write it.

*

NIGHT WALK, AUGUST 29

Smoldering sunset deep in August. I see myself in shadow against it. Mesquite rustles. Bats feed. The arroyo stays dry. I type this out on my phone. In my mind they are lines—telephone wires across sunset.

The light runs
like mercury I can't keep
up with it

I am not fast. I am not whole. I'm walking dusk slow. These suburban streets hum with air conditioners, will be our end. We are all writing the same poem. And the poem says: Please tell me how to make it stop. I keep walking

toward sunset. Stars stagger out. And don't do anything. There's a queen. There's a node. Three hawks patrol the neighborhood trees. We are all writing the same poem, and the poem says: The ground is so uneven. This street curls back on itself. What do I sound like when I talk about the dusk strung through palo verde leaves? I'm watching Scorpio watch you. That's just a start. What do I sound like when I try to explain how the stars refuse? We are all writing the same poem, and it says: I'm walking into the dry of the wash where things hide. There's another kind of knowledge I'm supposed to use. Tents billow along the parkway. People camp in the arroyo. There's a boarded-up house that no one can buy.

FALLS FIRST

I.

The sun spun like a coin on edge.

Mostly we worried about money,
about currents and the catch and the value
of the homes we lived in that the bankers owned.

Mostly we worried about the future.
In forest time, a river unwinds like the hem of a tulle dress,
but in our city hours, a river riots like a falcon, chides us
like an old bookkeeper
teaching us time and again we do not own it or what floats within.

We waded up to our ankles, knees, neck.

The moon pulls the current, a card trick,
the moon's up the river's sleeve.

To control the current is to control time is to control the exchange rate.

So we grabbed a girl,
by the wrist or waist, pulled her down
didn't let go, didn't have to pay her.

Heads or tails? The sun spun
away. Skin or scales?

We edged the ledger closer to shore.

2.

By the bank or on the coast
a girl might learn about seduction,
what to reveal or hide,
might learn about trauma
and trade, what will flood, what the currents will take
away, a girl might learn about pay and pay.

To drown is to be wrenched from your element, to be immigrant.

At certain latitudes at certain moments a child might lift
her face to take in the rain as if it were light

but a river is not wrought from light.

Anything that lives on water's surface knows how to stride, scurry, or improvise.
Anything that waits below knows who falls first.

MOTHER IS MATHEMATICIAN

Water in the gutter calculates, leaves that choke gutters run their equations. I look for a language to speak them. When I extend my arm, I feel a tourniquet of numbers, a hurricane under my left knee, tsunami calculations. Who did the math that caused me to see the spidered light of a live oak, birds trafficking without price tags or bar codes?

A wasp caught between window and screen dies on an equation. (But the view! O the view!) Like the economy that wasp would kill me. Equations feed cows, write folk songs, slip polyurethane between my mattress and me. Between dusk and the thin goblet of night—algorithms. Whatever frontage road, whatever utility poles hold up my story, these equations interstate. My life's a mile marker, a tag tied to a fencepost hemming a field of stones.

I swallow nickels to feed my child, while another mother eats pennies, while another eats Sacajawea dollars and spits out the ones that land on her tongue tail-side-up. Mother is mathematician, fucks calculating. I cannot get high enough

to see all the powers and parenthesis. Teach me the algorithms of carpets in convention centers, holes in the ground near Waxahachie. Chinese workers jump from factory windows in a fable writ with equations. I am a tired grammarian writing it out long hand on legal pads. Calculate "working class." Calculate "bohemian." We were always uncertain. Calculate "DIY." Calculate "sunset over the gas station." Mothers birth new math, parabola and pie graph, tell their children: *Listen!* to cicadas as unseen as numbers in the flickering trees,

Their song is the theorem that proves them.

TOWARD THE SHORELINE

As early as the 10th century, astute observers noted sunken trees fringed British coastlines, bare branches nearly tickling the water's surface at low tide mistaken for misplaced reflections or the tentative fingers of water nymphs beckoning from below the waves.

These sunken forests were thought

to be evidence of Noah's flood until the beginning of the 20th century, when the geologist Clement Reid proposed that "nothing but a change in sea level" accounted for the trees stretching from the high water mark "to the level of the lowest spring tide."

*

Plato first told the story of Atlantis, a city founded by a race of half-gods, half-mortals. Paradise. Until the inhabitants became greedy and bellicose. And the gods sent fire and earthquake to sink Atlantis into the sea.

*

When I became pregnant I watched birth videos because I had never witnessed an actual birth. Sitting on the floor of my doula's yoga studio, I was startled by the raw screams, moans that uncoiled into song, flood of blood and water

—how could any one hold so much?

*

Read back as far as Hippocrates and you find that women have always been always watery.

*

The Intergovernmental Panel on Climate Change predicts a rise in sea levels of 10–32 inches by the end of this century.

Water spilled on the ground cannot be gathered up.

*

A beautiful young woman stands naked at the shoreline in one birthing video, while the Black Sea laps at her thighs. Her equally beautiful friends hold her up like a crucified Jesus as she sways through her contractions.

In another, a woman recalls how she felt "all the power of the universe" spiraling through her during her son's birth. The film captures her in a mid-delivery orgasm.

I practiced spiraling and squatting and breathing through a variety of sensations.

But when my daughter dropped down into the birth canal, a clawing pain wrapped around my back and midsection for 15 hours. No chance to spiral or sing or breathe. When my water broke

my husband said he looked into my eyes and could not find me.

*

I like to tell people: I move to the desert and decide to write about water—which is not exactly true. Water

shifts, sloshes, spills, betrays form

—and what the water leaves behind?

a standard nail, a metal plaque, a painted sign.

*

On Wall Street the "high-water" mark refers to the highest peak in value reached by an investment fund/account, often used in the context of fund manager compensation, which is performance based.

Who tides? Who ebbs or floods?

*

During the last four periods of the Paleozoic, Arizona was ocean. Only the northeastern corner of the state remained above sea level.

In 2014 Arizona ranked ninth in the country for percentages of homes underwater.

In early 2024, roughly one out of every 37 homes in the United States was seriously underwater.

*

The birth video explained: "The quality of life will be defined by the quality of the birth."

The birth video explained that we could "move beyond the imprint of fear and suffering."

My husband and I studied many natural birthing techniques. By the time we thought to sign up for a childcare class, we were too late. We were never shown the proper way to diaper or perform infant CPR. When we brought our daughter home to an empty house, she cried all the time. She lost weight.

*

By 2018, approximately 9 percent of working families with children under the age of 6 were pushed out of the middle class because of childcare expenses. In the 1970s the median salary was $50,622 compared to $48,262 in 2010 (adjusted) while disposable income or anything not being spent on housing, healthcare, childcare, college in 1970s was $32,554 compared to $14,658 in 2010.

*

Every night I lie awake in bed listening to the sound of prerecorded waves playing on repeat from an iPod in my daughter's room.

Often when I sleep, I dream about money.

*

"The question whether to have children is of course prudential in part; it's concerned about what is or is not in one's own interests," explains one writer in *The New York Times*.

"But it is *also* an ethical question, for it is about whether to bring a person (in some cases more than one person) into existence — and that person cannot, by the very nature of the situation, give consent to being brought into existence."

*

Nearly every mother I know has trouble sleeping.

*

In the year of our drought, in the year of our marriage, all our favorite photographs were taken under cloud.

*

Turning his attention to a substance known as moorlog, dredged up from the bed of the North Sea in the early 20th century, geologist Clement Reid identified the compacted remains of bear, wolf, hyena, bison, mammoth, beaver, walrus, elk and deer as well as shells, wood, and lumps of peat. He concluded: "Noah's woods once extended far beyond the shore, occupying what is now the southern half of the North Sea, and stretching across to Holland and Denmark."

*

Scholars often insist that we're not meant to take accounts of Atlantis literally. "The idea is that we should use the story to examine our ideas of government and power," writes philosopher Julia Annas.

"We have missed the point if instead of thinking about these issues we go off exploring the sea bed."

*

The term "utopia" (from the Greek for "no-place/land") was coined by Sir Thomas More in his 16th-century work of fiction, inspired by Plato's Atlantis and travelers' accounts of the Americas.

On More's island of Utopia, private property doesn't exist. Houses (never locked) are rotated among the citizens every ten years. Everyone works the fields, training for at least two years in the countryside. People only work six hours a day

—and every household has two slaves.

*

One's utopia so quickly becomes another's flood.

*

I look to a reflection-heavy sea and can find no sky to correspond with the one that hangs above me. I look to the mirror of my daughter.

A real drowning looks nothing like they do on television. The victim usually can't scream, can't wave their arms, often can't lift their mouth above the water line

as the body sheds its technology.

*

Given that humankind is the most destructive species on the planet, philosopher David Benatar writes, "a life filled with good and containing only the most minute quantity of bad—a life of a single pinprick adulterated only by the pain of a single pin-prick—is worse than no life at all."

*

I want to teach my daughter how to swim, how to live off the grid, how to grow her own food and make her own art

but what I need to teach her how is how to die

or how to live as if she is already dead.

*

The woman whose house and husband and child were washed away by Hurricane Sandy explained: "You have to live all over again, in a different way."

USGS high water survey markers, driven into utility poles and tied with orange ribbons, flutter like a monk's robe.

It was raining when Mary Shelley began Frankenstein.

Tell me a story about water.

*

We moved to the desert for better jobs, no one should feel sorry for us.

We rent a three-bedroom house in hopes of putting 10 percent down on a 30-year mortgage if we can find something before interest rates rise.

*

"We are moving into a new era when science, technology, and spirituality are converging." In the video, children, toddlers—even infants—swim instinctively in gentle tides. "We can regain our authentic power," the video promises "and clear the pain of our ancestors from our system."

*

Underwater archeologists discover the ancient city, Heracleion, swallowed by the Mediterranean Sea and buried in sand and mud for more than 1,200 years.

They hoist bins of gold coins, Egyptian tablets, statues of gods, and anchors from the sea floor. Scientists theorize an earthquake may have caused the city with its large buildings to sink into waterlogged clay and sandy soil.

But it is unclear if it was a quick a disaster or a gradual abandonment

if people fled or simply turned away.

*

If I could have brought my daughter into "a world of love and safety" just by birthing her in water, or if her hospital birth could be the limit of all the damage that will be done to her, if I could buy the right cups for her to drink from to limit her exposure to BPA, if we could figure out whether to put our money in pensions or mutual funds or gold bars or a house, if buying local produce could end the collapse of bee colonies, if bicycling to work could short circuit the oil economy, if signing this petition could stop police brutality, if laying my body in the street or on the steps of the capitol could end brutality against immigrants, if withholding our taxes could stop the wars, if withholding our taxes could undo genocide, if we could short circuit the drone, if we could cut ourselves away, if we could either come clean or choke on our complicity.

I feel like those Greek women condemned to spend eternity in the underworld gathering water in a leaky jug or sieve.

*

We look out the window.

Do you see those clouds?

Yes, my daughter says, but it's not raining.

*

In another Atlantis-inspired myth, in the liner notes to their 1997 album *The Quest*, the African-American Detroit based techno duo, Drexciya, imagined a race of aquahumans born from the fetuses of pregnant slave women tossed into the Atlantic during the middle passage:

"Are Drexciyans water breathing, aquatically mutated descendants of those unfortunate victims of human greed? Have they been spared by God to teach us or terrorize us? Did they migrate from the Gulf of Mexico to the Mississippi river basin and on to the great lakes of Michigan?

Do they walk among us? Are they more advanced than us and why do they make their strange music?"

*

In this myth, no bins of gold coins or statues will be dredged up from the seabed

but far from shore, over a wall of sea, overboard, music rises from water-logged lungs

*

In the womb, a fetus's lungs fill with fluid and cannot supply oxygen to her body. The mother provides the fetus oxygen via the umbilical cord.

An infant's first breath usually happens at birth when she begins to cry.

*

first the sirens, then the water, then the water, then the water that falls, the bridge that falls the walls that fall, the house that floods the street that floods then the water then the water then the water

*

And after the flood, it's almost cliché to mention how fertile the soil.

To imagine Utopia is to admire the flower and remember that spring

is a season of hunger

is to make a wish and break the bone.

*

branch, blood, moorlog, estuaries, I looked into your reflection thick with leaves, broken surface, my stuttering reflection

be branch-felt gut, bring branch to surface, thirst, against the constraint of mud, sound it out, be knock-these-things-down, be mother-fucking mutable, rise, roil, foam, gather whatever you need, what stands in your way sweep aside, calculate by cubic feet, the pressure, power, learn this here in the desert, cover the surface with your surface, to hell with site specificity, seize every reflection, shatter, startle, reroute, rise, tide, sing

*

dear drowned, dear drowning, dear daughter

*

when the wood runs out, the bears move down the mountain
when you give a mouse a muffin, he demands so much more
all of the children's books teach economics
we put our spare change in a soup jar
coins from various currencies
make a sound like bell or a soft crash

*

To be the body sinking under the water's surface

under water everything becomes luminous
to understand your body because of water

to waiver like a penny underwater
can perhaps also teach us about an economy

What can we learn from this moment?

Not the drowning but what the drowned see.

MY DOCUMENTARIAN

tunes herself to the few
vowels mouthed by common sparrows, the ticks
and growls of systems around her. She holds
her landscapes up
to light like clicking through a View
-Master, to re-inscribe relations
between the landscape
and the I. She grows over soil she's tasted.

She winds string through fingers, spools
a circuit for our grief.
                    She *quipus* in lieu
of standard accounting practices, takes care
to be non-compliant. She archives, she file folders.
Field and forest blur, data falls like ash around her.
She records, too, a hand on her doorknob, light
on the lawn. My documentarian pulls a thread,
knots unloosen in her.

For a year no water ran
in the riverbed,
still we called it river. She ponders these betrayals,
remembers the brain is built on analogy, on smears
and turns. A mail truck drives past her house,
and she feels her debts.
My documentarian

tilts the page away from spreadsheet
toward police binders and microfiche, coffee
and billboard prayers. Her archive scrolls like
a time-lapse sunset, sings like a jar of breath.
A tree in her yard throws lines
of sun barb and shade,
just to her porch steps.
Her poems extend.

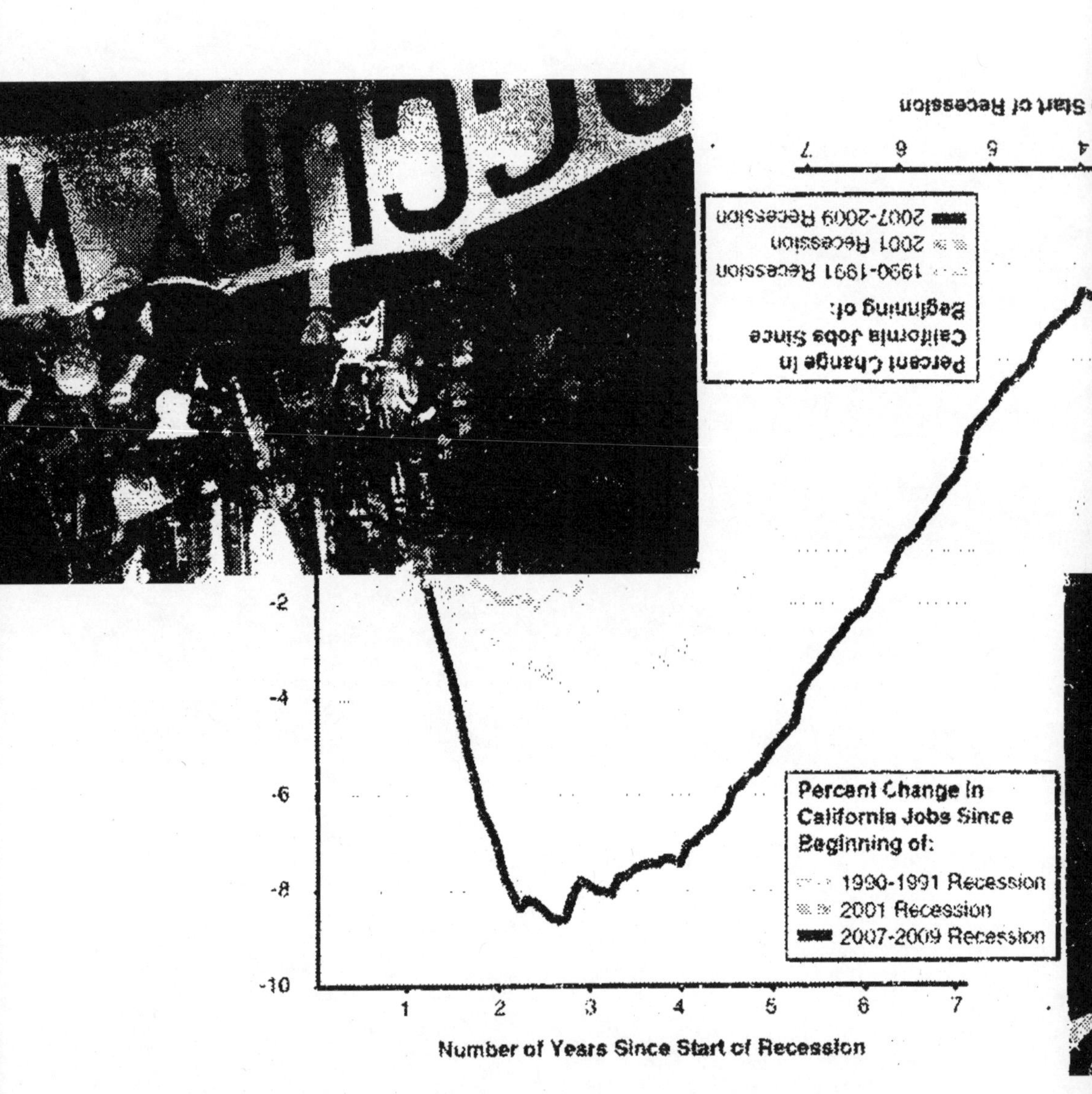

Percent Change in California Jobs Since Beginning of:
1990-1991 Recession
2001 Recession
2007-2009 Recession
-2
-4
-6
-8
-10
1
2
3
4
5
6
7
Number of Years Since Start of Recession

UTOPIA MINUS

The zero panorama seemed to contain ruins in reverse, that is—all the new construction that would eventually be built. This is the opposite of the "romantic ruin" because the buildings don't fall into ruin after they are built but rather rise into ruin before they are built. This anti-romantic mise-en-scène suggests the discredited idea of time and many other "out of date" things. But the suburbs exist without a rational past without the "big events" of history.... A Utopia minus a bottom, a place where the machines are idle, and the sun has turned to glass...

Robert Smithson, "A Guide to the Monuments of Passaic New Jersey"

UP THE ROAD

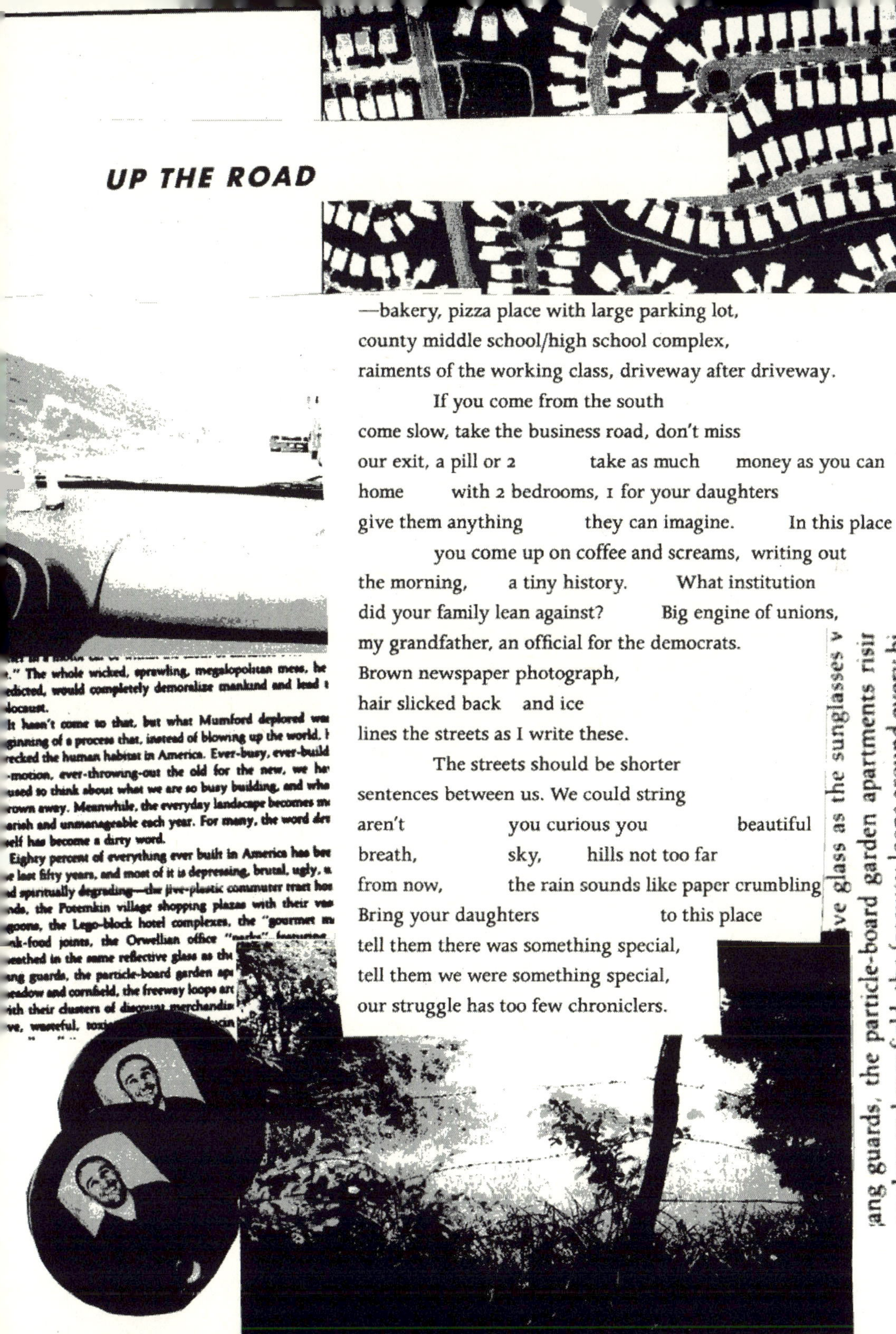

—bakery, pizza place with large parking lot,
county middle school/high school complex,
raiments of the working class, driveway after driveway.
    If you come from the south
come slow, take the business road, don't miss
our exit, a pill or 2   take as much   money as you can
home   with 2 bedrooms, 1 for your daughters
give them anything   they can imagine.   In this place
    you come up on coffee and screams, writing out
the morning,   a tiny history.   What institution
did your family lean against?   Big engine of unions,
my grandfather, an official for the democrats.
Brown newspaper photograph,
hair slicked back   and ice
lines the streets as I write these.
    The streets should be shorter
sentences between us. We could string
aren't   you curious you   beautiful
breath,   sky,   hills not too far
from now,   the rain sounds like paper crumbling
Bring your daughters   to this place
tell them there was something special,
tell them we were something special,
our struggle has too few chroniclers.

WOODSMOKE, STARBUCKS, GETTYSBURG

You say smoke follows a fire's tender, and all morning the fire stalks me, throwing up facefuls of cloud and ash to make me feel far from myself in the mountains of Chiapas or a cabin in New Hampshire tucked into another's skin, where my legs might be longer, my thighs might be broader, where I feel axeblade and muscledwarm throughout winter.

But we are here, wrapped in our customary weather: cedar and live oak, flock of windchimes over Bee Creek, a pipe organ in some vague cathedral of wood parasite and pebble. I build a fire in the rusted potbellied stove that you dragged from the hill to your deck. Great furnace of twig and newspaper. And even when we pass into full afternoon, I do not stop. You joke that you will slay a deer for me to roast.

Instead, we drive into town past construction cranes on the river, floodwalls of condominiums. The Sunglass Hut on the Drag has been boarded up. And outside what was once Peet's Coffee, someone has scrawled: *More than this?* Now there is a Diesel, now there is a Pita Pit. You tell me that the corporate plan for Starbucks was not efficiency but ubiquity, so that whenever we think coffee we think Starbucks.

Tonight when I smell woodsmoke, I think of amputees under Civil War trees, Antioch, Gettysburg. You can travel to Georgia: fields of flags and Popeye's Chicken where Sherman burned plantations.

Our dog looks for bigger refineries, lays in full sun. A squirrel chatters in a sycamore tree. The broken boat on the hillside makes an impossible shipwreck, another history.

O Sunglass Hut, we hardly knew you!

NOTES FROM THE LAST GREAT CIVIL WAR STORY

Our dog licks my teacup;
late dog
days of summer, I study
new urbanism, racial
uprisings, cultural memory,
patterns of glassworks
on some foreign field of sand,
"high mortality events."
Death makes such a blunt box
such a 24-hour news channel,
video of a cypress tree
which refuses to grow
while a window
around the screen
goes from dark to light,
day to night.

Gen. Sherman's
funeral, Feb. 21, 1891, St. Louis,
cold as the chill that filled
the general's lungs.
Former Confederate
Gen. Joseph Johnston,
vanquished at Appomattox,
removes his hat as the cortège
passes, saying Sherman
would have done no less,
dies of pneumonia
2 weeks later.

Woke this morning in Dallas
with Bentonville, NC
written on my palm.

NAIL GUNS IN THE MORNING

Nail guns in the morning from the street behind my house,
Outside: tin roof, cement tabletops, "vast maw of modernity" (Sontag),
the UPS man, someone has painted all of my windows shut.

The study of trauma comes shortly after the steam engine,
an affliction known as "railway spine," characterized by headaches,
fatigue, difficulty in breathing, reduction of sexual potency, stammering, cold sweats.

Report from Charles Dickens, June 1865, after train wreck:
    Wakes up in sudden alarm. Dreams much.

Storms this afternoon in Dallas
in the parking lot of the Target/Best Buy/Payless Shopping Center,
big chalices of rain, contusioned sky over the east, big yellow bus moving north
toward the dark end of—what?—

this weather, this fiscal year, this end of empire during which I am reading
the circulars stuck in my screen door, ice waiting
in the highest breath of atmosphere. It will get to us.

I am patient on the living room couch, let water drain from
the kitchen sink. Last night over dirty dishes, I told Farid
I would never write a poem that just said: *Stop the War*.

So frequently, I want a witness. Sit with me,
C. Dickens, let me tell you how bad
the food is on Amtrak, how a Pullman position
was a plum job for a freedman, how stevedores once owned the city
hall, how bandits shot through the windows of the smoking car.

Stop the war, stop the war, stop the war, stop the war, stop the war.

CHALKMARKS ON THE FRONT WALK

Calendula by the curb an empty watering can

As I pull him across the lawn, the toddler
holds on to one side of his wagon
cups his balls with the
other hand

Autumn wren on a telephone wire. A sliver
less of each day. What's next?

From a bird by the hydrant, 3 trills, the last 1 clipped.

on the wall by the fireplace
we can fill it   with stones,
flowers, toenails, pebbles
of shit   or scat   or something
else Anglo-Saxon   and indispensable.
No books on Texas   birds, no
botany, the rock is called
a batholith, stands 1825 feet,
a large, solid granite dome
where white men
fled captivity, Comanche,
Tonkawas, a sword-edged
tongue or a nettle you carry for miles.
    At night the rock moans its way
from hot to cold.
Grasses by the highway grow bovine.
What is happening there? a harvest of lime?
In our luminous day by day,
the poem was
a record of presence, attention. Music
rises from the deep lobes of lung.
    Your turn to tend,
to imagine first a settlement
then something else, to wish
to remark ancestrally,
to note in the deepbook a scent
of sewage or sulfur, while wading
the tall grass toward the goats
penned in our neighbors' backyard.
Self-reflective, palms open. I never want
to bother anyone with my presence,
    (*my, my, my, my, my*)
not even the goats. The fire pitches
its guttural song, wind makes its way
through the porchwood,

movement in the musical sense, not transit.
I rake the fire's hair, the grate
heats, a rib cage, pubic bone.
        A treaty of non-aggression
between the Comanche
and the first German settlers
became the only such agreement
in Texas never broken by the Texans,
thus the guttural tongue, the fire
that moves to its end. I am tired
of tending and my thighs grow cold.
"I take SPACE to be
the central fact to man born in America,
from Folsom cave to now . . .
Large and without mercy" (Charles Olson).
        On the edge of the creek
2 or 3 yellow flowers out of season,
A small earthmover, a shovel, when I asked
her to name the trees—she looked shocked
—scrub oak not worth anything.
Does one need to tend a war?
Night catches first in the thicket
above the farmhouse, stones by the creek
moonglow against the field, help me
name these constellations:
        cricket, lawn chair, ledger, rake.
All day, I watch
the fire from the couch, but should have turned
the armchair, tended the window,
dragged a kitchen chair
to the porch,
watched the wall-mounted mountain
goat high above the kitchen cabinet, Capricorn,
        eyes to the roof,
your eyes so much better than mine,

so self-fixed, so specimen still.
You lack nothing.
        I wander
the window. Large but never empty
never ours.

DEAR MR. SURGEON GENERAL

Lately every time I drive over a suspension bridge, I feel myself at a steely end, walking a knife blade, subject to winds, looking east as if calling out to the dead.

Purple clover along a highway is blood on my fingers.

And sometimes, Sir, I cry after sex, my mind like a plastic bag tumbling down Kent Street edging the East River, water tankers, maintenance plants; my mind roving the white line of a pockmarked road: soiled and mute, beyond touch or notice.

Once climate and geography were thought to cure illness. Rilke knew this and wrote: " . . . I left Paris, tired and quite sick, and traveled to this great northern plain, whose vastness and silence and sky ought to make me well again."

But where, Sir, might I go to await my convalescence?

When the Williamsburg Bridge rises up into view, sometimes a sigh will blow through a teamster. Sometimes you'll see a fly in an elevator like a feeling that has no place. You might wonder if it is some cycle of weather.

"Sex is difficult," Rilke explains.

One winter I lived in Williamsburg, Brooklyn. From my kitchen table, I could see the spire of the Chrysler Building peeking over the roof of an evangelical church. My roommate practiced martial arts. In order to test her threshold for pain, she never tapped off an opponent when trapped in a difficult move. At the foot of the bridge, National Guardsmen shivered in tents, while her arms purpled with bruises.

Some nights we drank licorice tea and talked about our mothers. Some nights snow blew in over the East River, leaving the Chrysler Building's spire to flail like a compass needle. Most nights I fell asleep to the clattering chains of a padlock coiling and uncoiling from a gate.

Dear Mr. Chairman of Ethics, Leadership and Personnel Policy in the U.S. Army's Office of the Deputy Chief of Staff for Personnel

First, let me explain: My mother forbade me to walk fence rails with the Maleski boy. She barred me from taking off my shirt to dig flowerbeds with the Holloway girl. I kicked an overturned coffee can in the middle of the cul-de-sac. Storm after storm blew past the screen door. Standing under the plum tree's pale pink blossoms was putting on a veil.

In the hard soil of childhood, God was everywhere: in pitted sycamores, a vibrating clothes line, in fireflies hung still as lanterns from a Japanese maple.

One day I carved a whole landscape in the windowsill. Sun, willow, car, lady. Perhaps there were rabbits. My mother grabbed my wrist; rains broke; livewires writhed like eels through our streets.

How much loneliness must we inherit?

So, Sir, I grew earth-bound and cursed: a quarry, a construction site. God lagged behind in the pale light of swimming pools and pines. I took lovers and planes. In the desert east of Palm Springs, I drove past windmills flapping like angels trying to redirect traffic.

Yes, that was me kneeling down

to take a birth control pill

by baggage claim area three.

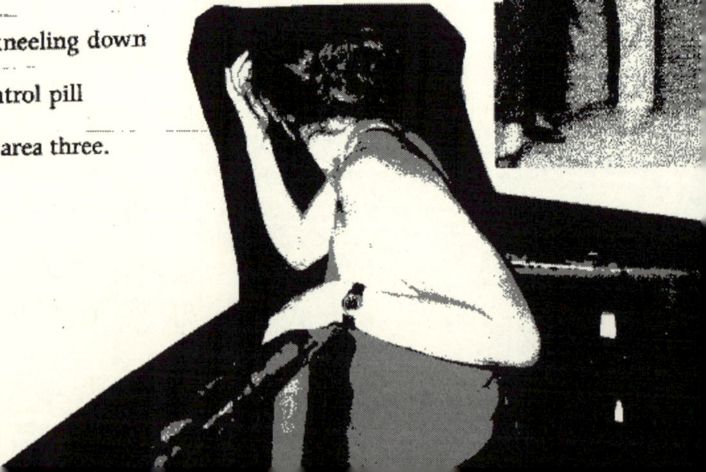

Shoshana Felman explains culturally traumatic events require "a positive
necessity of accounting" instead of articulation or confession. (153). She cites
Walter Benjamin's idea of "translation" as a possible metaphor for a

Of course, Sir, I can see it clearly now. Where once there was a thicket, I recognize three trees. A complicated song: a cardinal's call, a mother's voice, a wedding march. I want to undo it. Wind brings one bush to thrash and panic while another remains still as porcelain. Promiscuity, like a season, has its limits. Inevitably, rain weaves a sort of loose net on the window screen. Any woman of a certain age will recognize it as cheap lace.

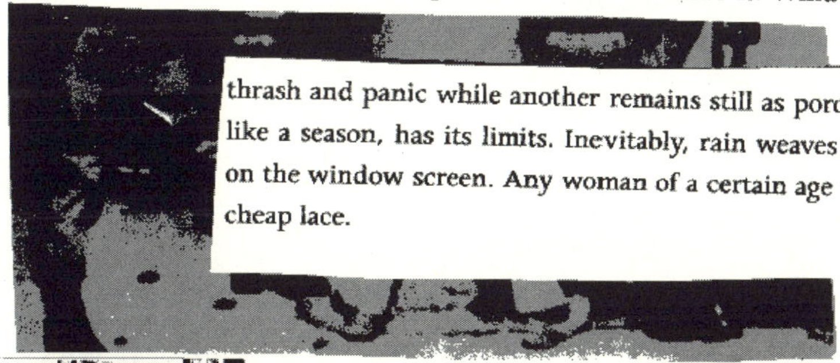

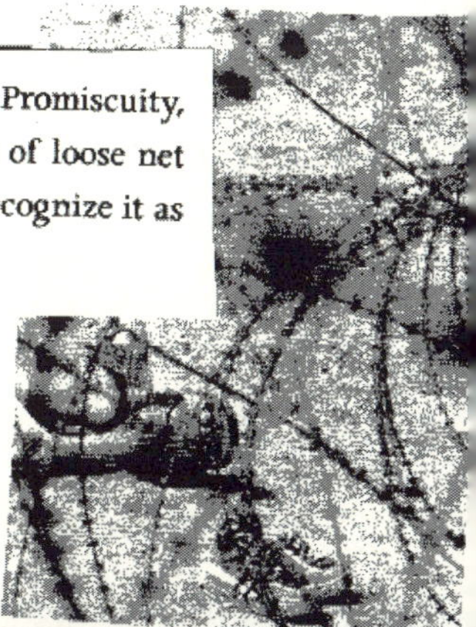

ISABELLA

The problem is that I always want two
things at once: to linger on Egyptian cotton sheets
and to be up at my desk hard drive whirring;
to sit on the dock dangling my feet in Eagle Lake
and simultaneously to be writing you this letter
about the ripples I send clear to the far bank,
how my toes hang above reeds and tadpoles,
about the family of geese that came on shore
yesterday afternoon and shit everywhere.

I am learning to row. Winds blow from the west.
An oar can act as brake or motor.
The ribs of the boat make a cradle.

Last night's sleep was shallow, and I dreamt
I flung myself over a group of children
with arms spread until my winter jacket
opened to wings. Men torched
parked cars. Police hurled grenades
across a street. And while we huddled
behind a Gap advertisement near a subway
entrance, my father ran toward
the barricades calling
another woman's name.

ROBERT MUELLER MUNICIPAL AIRPORT

And now you are flying, airborne in the thick
white sky, shedding gravity like an accent,
like a way you used to sign your name.

I lean back in your chair, put on your hat,
press your water glass to my lips.

Rain falls over the lake.

At the city's new airport, you empty
your pockets: a kind of downpour,
a little divorce: everyone can see
what's inside, an agent takes your file,
your nail clippers, a small pair of scissors.

The x-ray machine reduces your contents
to the barest geometries, cartoon lightning
in a little box of storm.

Rain smells of rocks and concrete,
makes the air fat, makes the dock
on the lake disappear into a gray road,
nearly metallic, the color of something
that could be "used as a weapon"
something federally disapproved.

Once I left a man, a marriage, a country;
I picked up a new accent wherever I went.

You say goodbye, empty your pockets,
everyone reads their contents, and everyone
can see into the buildings of the abandoned airport
through a fence around the parking lot:

the baggage claim is still as a stone heart.
And no one knows what we might build there,
no one reads the words that graffiti artists leave
in silver spray paint.

BIG IDEAS

: this skyline these boats
on the corps of engineers' lake, glassy view
        and your eyes gray.

In this season nothing changes
not sky nor traffic,   the neighbor
          who lets his dogs shit in our yard.

You put the wet towels in the hamper, I told you
not to put wet towels in the hamper.

Dead summer just a pause   ripe/rot:
the light turns on the same
          but day goes out a little earlier.

          End of the workweek: a cartoon steak
pulled by a cartoon string.

I'm talking about the weather, brother,
      and it ain't getting better.

MIDSTATE

There are no great cities left in America. Take Dallas, gateway to the West. Its skyline rises from the prairie trimmed in neon, insecure. In Austin, one evening, sitting in friends' reupholstered vintage living room, Farid confessed his passion for the *Real Housewives of the OC*: their personal trainers, their cosmetic surgeries, their luxury SUVs. Farid and I come from the working class. "What would be the male equivalent of breast implants?" our friend Phillip mused. The Dallas skyline edged in neon.

One August, I took a train to Buffalo from New York City: my marriage in shreds by June; my lover back to his wife by late July. On the train to Buffalo, I carried a bottle of Herradura, a gift from the lover recently returned from Mexico. For 10 hours, the train shuddered and lurched: palisades, can't-sit-through emptiness of midstate, dining-car Styrofoam. I arrived in Buffalo at sunset. Big cathedral of rust at city's edge: old railway station, sky the color of aged tequila, a pony glass of late-summer light. But it wasn't a train station at all. It was a stockyard, a Walmart distribution center, a floating casino. It was a skate park for a while in the 1980s. It was an opera house dedicated on the 15th day of November, in this the year of the Dixie cup, in the year of the orange construction cone.

The bodies of my days open up
in the garden
of
my memory,
America

Do you think Berrigan was talking about sex or monuments?

Austin is a mid-sized American city smug with bumper stickers: "Dog is my co-pilot" and "Visualize Whirled Peas." After a long drive through central Texas, I stopped to piss in an Austin coffee shop/bakery. Graffiti in the pink stall read: *Men fall in love with the women they are attracted to. Women become attracted to the men they love.* And under that, scrawled in black sharpie: *White People Suck.* Austin has a large percentage of white people.

You might think the ruined cathedral a symbol for marriage. You might think the ruined train station some Tintern Abbey. Cars stalled in the freight yard. You might think that both Ted Berrigan and I should know better. Recently, I have lost a gold bracelet, a stone from a Mexican ring, my ATM card. My bumper has been tied to my car with string. In bathrooms on interstates from New Jersey to San Antonio, I have read graffiti: *Big Hairy Pussies Rule, Vote John Kerry, Bitch! Wipe the Seat.*

Manhattan has become the casino version of itself. Chicago is cold brick. San Francisco is water spilling from a glass.

Once I tried to avoid Dallas, turned east at Corsicana, found myself in rows of cotton surprised in the flat morning light to find that we still grew anything in fields so vast and monotonous.

Once Farid and I drove west from Dallas to see the coast of the prairie. Cars paused at a 4-way intersection; the unimaginably wide lanes of a new subdivision stretched toward the government lake. 3 water towers, wide bridge and the gray-blue line of horizon, commerce in the black-eyed Susans.

A stalled car shone from road's dark edge; a river ran dry three-quarters through the fields, marked by cottonwoods. Little gash, little Suez. Farid stopped at a gas station off the highway. Standing at the urinal, he thought he saw the work of rot or age. But what looked like mildew in the grout between tiles was actually penmanship from men who'd been there, listing birthplace, hometown, way station, destiny: *Tulsa, Odessa, Abbott, Waxahachie.*

YELLOW FINCHES DROP FROM A PLANE TREE

Crosses of sunlight burn through the sugar maple
each afternoon in little crucifixions.

Blue-black lake like an 8-mm film,
its name means "high winds"
in a language not spoken by the original inhabitants.

How does a tree move when it is angry?
I want to be angry like that.

DEAR MADAM SECRETARY OF NATIONAL SECURITY

All day the tatters of a hurricane blow overhead: black swaths of thunder and slicing rain, marble swirls of cloud. Grass brightens against gray. Steers call back. A cardinal and his mate worry through the possum haw. On a fence post, she preens. She cocks her head and calls. He flits and glides, carrying sunflower seeds from the picnic table to her orange beak. And when the rains return, they thread their way further into the ailanthus tree.

The Ladies Birthday Almanac warns: "Weaning children should be done when the moon is in Sagittarius or Capricorn...Do not cut a nerve when Mercury is afflicted."

Last night I dreamt of a porcelain dinner plate. I turned over small bones, picking at caramel-colored meat, my fork discovering the rust and gray tail feathers of that female cardinal I have been watching for days. I carried the plate into the kitchen to accuse. The cook turned and threw her dishrag, shaking her head, shouting to someone else as she walked down the hall. My stomach grew sour and sore.

Madam, do you ever get the feeling there's something wrong with how things are run? Parents bury their children by the dozen under US-made bombs. Tropical depressions spiral through the afternoon. And when a cardinal spits out his high, hard song, I feel responsible to him as well.

What a time, then, to be an American in love! *The Ladies Birthday Almanac* warns: "Never plant under barren signs...Cut timber in the Old of Moon."

What a time then, Madam, to feel the cool remorse of dusk, when cornrows sway uneasily in the backyard, when a bull's cry resembles the sounds of a branch as it breaks.

DEAR MR. DIRECTOR OF THE CENSUS BUREAU

Yesterday, hundreds of broadwing hawks moved in kettles over eastern Travis County, dropping shadows on scaly pines and glassphalt drives, powerlines and watering holes, sailing in currents of rise and fall, heavenly, purgatorial.

This morning outside the Spider House cafe, a manager strings white lights through rungs of jasmine. At a table near mine, a girl sits with her mother and boyfriend. The girl pulls handfuls of bread from a plastic bag. "Tell us the story about the night she was born," the boy asks.

A cement mixer grinds across the street. On the sidewalk, a woman struggles with a sac of laundry.

"I was playing Risk," the girl's mother explains, "and they were letting me win."

Dante described the universe as a series of spheres and heavens: sphere of air and fire, heaven of moon and venus, heaven of fixed stars, angelic circles, rose of the blessed.

My mother hung curtains on the morning of my birth. My father untangled strands of tinsel. Capricorn ascended. I want to chart all the satellites dangling like a mobile above my hospital nursery.

Hawks alight on a high-voltage tower by the highway. Each scrub oak below them opens like a flower. Each city block unfolds like a square on a game board. This morning I can see the staggering boundaries of power grids and aquifers. But, Sir, they tell me nothing.

Sphere of the chain-link fence around a daycare center. Purgatory of police cars pulling up to the curb. Heaven of winter treetops, barren and brittle; rose of the boy in a paper hat running toward the crosswalk.

BIG THEORY

A red woodpecker scales the live oak, while I sleep, the phone
rings   makes its erasures:
        a demolition/construction
        a dream in which I'm revising a list with my father—gone
        the way of whole neighborhoods in the Bronx.

                Robert Moses shrugs his concrete shoulders
                        Robert Moses, I say, *drop the knife.*

In the summer of 2001, I lived in the Bowery, took photographs of police
call boxes,

took the train through Newark, NJ: warehouse, community college, broadface
    of the projects irregardless of choices. I was a lonely child, loved looking
at things no one would notice: Rahway,   Linden,   Elizabeth:
the many-eyed, bricked-up, gold-domed, on the platform waiting.

So far as we feel sympathy, we think we are not accomplices.

Thick rain and tree roots knuckle the sidewalk.
        In Bloomfield, NJ, the sidewalks were slate gray, dark as thunderheads
big bang   big theory   of charge/discharge.

As a child, I thought I could save my mother's life by stepping in front of her.

OTHER DENVER ECONOMIES

Green tree in the yard and a dog
so skinny he fits through
the fence rails, tulips and the fence
that splits the tree.
Little white birds
of this season
of circulars, children
walk home from school
where they sit in a second
language. And the hands they hold
smell of bleach. Spring is a chorus
in the helicopter's throat, the back
yard's muddy lyric; April is long division.
You'll find neighborhoods so poor
economists can't figure out an equation
for how a mother feeds her children.
Wage puzzle, they call it. Hello, season
of WIC, SSIs, AFDCs.   So sweet
these chairs on porches. Drink a whole glass
of tap water, consider the spool
of cassette tape dangling from a branch.
Watch the small yellow school bus, inside a boy
rides strapped in a wheelchair, everyone
else in their pick-up trucks and SUVs.
Keep them moving, please. Barefoot sister on the porch
holding a black leather belt
          —you can make up whatever story you want.
I've got my stockings in my purse, bird in the gutter, butterfly
on the stoop. No—that's a moth. Anyway, she looked fine
to me. There are other economies
in Denver. At a sex club on S. Broadway,
women pay a $20 cover, but couples pay upwards of $50,
and a single man might pay $100 or more
depending on the night. Most of the time
we think of the body as fixed

in value—I've been 5'4" for years now.
Most of the time we don't think of the body
and the soul satellites. Across the street
a Labrador sits in an open doorway,
the oak tree still clutches its autumn leaves
while its crown blossoms green.
It's not like any of us.

THE END OF ANOTHER CREATURE

Starlings in the magnolia tree crackle, static, lightning; a helicopter floats overhead. Harvest brings dove-hunting season, a great migration. For six days I watch monarch butterflies scatter across the Metroplex, dream their carcasses onto the highway, dream black beetles biting my fingers in your clasped hands. I feel a pilot light at the back of my throat, while the helicopter groans a few blocks deeper down Ross Avenue. And the magnolia tree falls silent, and the season concludes.

The Market migrates; the Market scatters across the Metroplex.
The Market dreams my carcass onto the highway, groans a few
blocks deeper into my neighborhood.

In the liquidity of late afternoon sun, a truck on the avenue clips branches from elms. What policy might we bring forth on our front-yard folding table? Deposit insurance? The return of Glass Steagall? Pull over. Price what you see. Privatize this rush-hour traffic. Look disappointed. The helicopter answers: pulse, pulse, pulse. These fences make a triangle, a shed of mostly shadow and quiet behind the boxwoods where someone left chemicals.

DEAR MR. PRESIDENT

High above 38th Street, city workers on cherry-picker trucks unwind cables thick as a man's arm. They uproot telephone poles. Steel columns, twice as tall as treetops, bank over our heads like a storm front. Grackles percolate through live oaks.

What gears maneuver above us shielded by billboards and cloud?

My brother takes measurements of unoccupied buildings. In vacated spaces, the mind counts ceiling tiles, makes its own partitions. Once, he found dozens of dead pigeons fallen on the gray carpeting of a third floor. They had slipped in through a hole in the roof. For days, they must have flown panicked through corridors and stairwells, under slack wires and cold fluorescent lighting. Regardless of where they lay, maggots eventually spindled inside them.

Mr. President, I want you to understand this is not a parable. In interminable expanses, God is a barbed-wire fence. Here in Texas, storms blow in from the west, plump with lightning and loosed leaves, tugging at raincoats, ripping dust from roads. Kudzu vines darken on the hillside; blue jays tear an afternoon to rags.

But, Sir, no matter what promise of voltage hangs overhead, a storm is a hand brushed over velvet: fields of emerald grass return to gold, a kind of wealth too large for a pocket or windshield.

Tonight, all the utility lines above 38th Street glisten like bronze threads hemming in strip malls and practice fields, vapor trails soaring over intersections. And pigeons swerve from north to east stained by a red light that resembles an emergency exit's glow.

A LETTER TO EILEEN MYLES

Tonight I want to write Eileen Myles. Eileen, I want to say, do you think I should have a baby? I am forty. I ask everybody I know and even some (like you) whom I don't. I ask the Pulitzer Prize-winning poet Robert Hass in the parking lot of an Italian American deli in east Dallas. And when I pose the question I feel I am on a great ship slicing through the Atlantic. The sun cuts a rut across the ocean, a divot. Nothing seems impossible, just far away. Robert Hass says: Oh, you are trying to decide. That's difficult. We drive Robert Hass north of Dallas to Archer City. High school kids take prom pictures in front of the courthouse. Maybe it's the county seat. Robert Hass spots a scissortail flycatcher on a telephone wire. We drink sodas at the Sonic because the Dairy Queen has gone out of business. O Walter Benjamin! O Larry McMurtry and all of your beautiful cowboys who did not have to worry about babies!

I've been sad, I want to tell Eileen. I've been spinning around with a decision decided. A body may be finished, but the mind strains. Farid and I have $15,000 in savings, $40,000 in debt. In 40 years, we've seen privatizations, a loss of price cautions, a rise in sunblock. Trees know how to make more of this flat gray light across the prairie.

I grew up in suburban New Jersey. My father took the train to work in "the city." My mom had a part-time job. We spun our skateboards around the cul-de-sac, gathered at the park at dusk. We smoked cigarettes and pot. When I went to sleep, an air conditioner in the window frame clicked and hummed.

Now the city won't have me. I have gone to market; I have gone on the market. I want to come to you, Eileen. Others have offered suggestions. One poet has a chicken coop; another grows kombucha colonies in her kitchen cabinets, she wants to raise goats. Another wants to go to Maine to study the contemporary back-to-the-land movement. What do you make of our economic avant-garde? We work in state institutions; we work for private high schools; we work in offices with views to airconditioning equipment on roofs.

Farid and I do not have time, do not have wealthy parents, no Girl Scouting skills, no collection of Foxfire books. One year we lived in a cabin on an Austin creek. A snake coiled under the sink. Day after day we hauled bags of garbage and laundry up a hillside. We were going to learn plumbing and carpentry. Instead we took our plastic rafts to the dirty water, watched the sun drop through sycamore trees. The creek became a mechanism of documentation and invisibility. No one ever knew what nested on its banks. When the winter came, we shivered near a space heater. When squirrels crawled into the roof, we left for a duplex in Dallas, where Bonnie met Clyde, where George married Mary Oppen.

Once I asked the MacArthur award–winning poet CD Wright about children. CD Wright said: Don't worry. These days you can buy a baby on eBay. But if we eBayed the baby, Eileen, we would still have to pay $7,500 a year for day care. We'd still have to find money for a down payment, replace our 10-year-old cars, plan our retirement. We are young and in love, all the movies say, we have everything. Farid says money rises as if a tall field of wheat; step in and it closes around you. Just beyond the window of our car traveling south down the North Dallas Tollway. No, that's corn. No, that's weeds.

11 RAILWAY LINES STRETCH FROM CHICAGO BY 1861

an adolescent daughter slutting around
showing off   her terrible,   a pine tree
gone rusty   in wintertime,   sun
seeps under her sweater,
the gravel turns   to asphalt
and the farmland opens up to cars
        deracinated country folk
could be wooed
by dollar stores, wind turbines
two tree trunks grope and bind
when you slice off a piece of crazy tail,
he warns me, know what the fence post knows
you can drive
for an hour south of Charlottesville
watch a skinny girl walk a long
road recently paved, tar clings to fence weeds,
worried about loyalty
        unmoored from the nation
the thickly accented philosopher explained
we could find hope   rich light
on the stable roof
a boy from down the road
who will read her differently
who steps out of the trees responsible
for love, under a system that pays him
no mind   no heed   no blossoms
yet on the redbud
but space cleared for their coming

ALEXANDER LITVINENKO

I found a billiard ball in the dirt next to the driveway
a tear-off, a throw-away, a non sequitur awaiting me this good-natured morning
beside the neighbor's rusted fence post.
Inside her yard I found room for all of us.
Move the planter to the steps, watch the snow melt from the eaves.
Can someone reach the wind chimes, clear their throat as if beginning
    a ceremony?
    We sip
unstable atoms in every cup of tea, fields of ice melt at the polar caps.
Find a blanket to lay upon them, a lead-thick thing like those thrown over a lap
by an x-ray technician before he slips from the room, flips a switch,
a circuit completed/broken   bones   as white as a silence
as when   returning from work,
    we reach the top of the stairs, call out: "Is anyone home?" Every day

another source of heat expires, bones from another
century. Winter bends
the porch flowers, stills the wind chimes, kills the vine growing
through the chain-link.

If you swallow the right pill
your blood will glow inside of you, if they inject the right dye
it is possible to perceive any corporeal surface, a customs agent
flashing his light beneath our car, checking the contents.
    Where do you want to see?
Imagine watching your own blood switch back its course
round a bend, remake its banks, there
by the river in the darkest soil we might build a city,
erect a barbed-wire fence,
    use any means to defend it.

Nerve agents, poison and window falls. Kremlin foes have been attacked or killed over the years

The spy, who had fled Russia for London, dictated a widely trumpeted statement just before his death. He fingered Putin. "You may succeed in silencing me, but that silence comes at a price," Alexander Litvinenko said. "... The howl of protest from around the world will reverberate, Mr. Putin, in your ears for the rest of your life."

Within days, Putin questioned that letter's authenticity, calling it "political provocation." But this letter wasn't the whole of Litvinenko's final remarks. He also gave detailed interviews to British authorities — comments that have, until Tuesday, remained sealed.

WHAT DOES A POSTMODERN POEM LOOK LIKE?
WHAT DOES A POST NEW YORK SCHOOL POEM LOOK LIKE?
WHERE DOES LYRIC MEET LANGUAGE?

90s
theory - 90s
→ deconstruction
postmodern
↳ narratives
metanarratives
- self. construction
- stable construct

rarely unlocks the door and enters, dusts off the shelves, forgets what the neighbors think long enough to find out what it's like to live there. I have a preconception in the book I'm writing, that there is a unified self and that the pronoun "I" is a word which should be given back to people, who need it, but deepened. However I'm living in the house of that preconception as openly as I can, pointing at the furniture, occasionally breaking the knick-knacks and spilling espresso or Contrex on the rugs. I'm trying to say what I know and I'm finding that honesty is difficult, interesting, and unexpected. The more I write this cover about self-censorship, that it has mo

Mother, are not symbolic but real, autobiographical. It is also and equally clear that this poem, while it uses bits of persona detail and elements of story is not about the poet's life. The poem is not about anything she is using to make the poem.

Much has been made of the transition from lyric to narrative, from metaphor to allegory, from seduction to possession, from incantation to realism. Yet despite the constant intrusion of new genres and new media, lyric persists. Is it possible to have a culture without it? "The poem and you need each other" is how Guest expresses this. From reading the works presented here, I have learned much about how lyric might be an ideal genre for certain sorts of critique, and how the lyric space of intimacy has the potential to be an exemplary space for examining political intimacies, race and gender intimacies, and community intimacies in addition to its relentless attention to more personal intimacy. Berssenbrugge writes of a ... space that is larger and more fertile for me than writing

The postmodern critique of "identity," though relevant for renewed black liberation struggle, is often posed in ways that are problematic. Given a pervasive politic of white supremacy which seeks to prevent the formation of radical black subjectivity, we cannot cavalierly dismiss a concern with identity politics. Any critic exploring the radical potential of postmodernism as it relates to racial difference and racial domination would need to consider the implications of a critique of identity for oppressed groups. Many of us are struggling to find new strategies of resistance. We must engage decolonization as a critical practice if we are to have meaningful chances of survival even as we must simultaneously cope with the loss of political grounding which made radical activism more possible. I am thinking here about the postmodernist critique of essentialism as it pertains to the construction of "identity" as one example.

promptly forget. I hate to see someone whose ... *taken* by someone whose careerist intentions are obscene. Sim I feel discouraged when the country is too incestuous defensive to recognize the living intelligence of the city. I aim to carry the smoked ham of my voice to Beulahland. I do not intend to write as though I had not gotten wind of "this here" or "that there" semiotic theory, regardless of which if any one theory prevails.

ANSWER THESE QUESTIONS IN TURN, ONE IN THE FORM OF POETRY AND THE OTHER IN THE FORM OF PROSE:

WHAT DID YOU INHERIT?

WHAT DO YOU REPRODUCE?

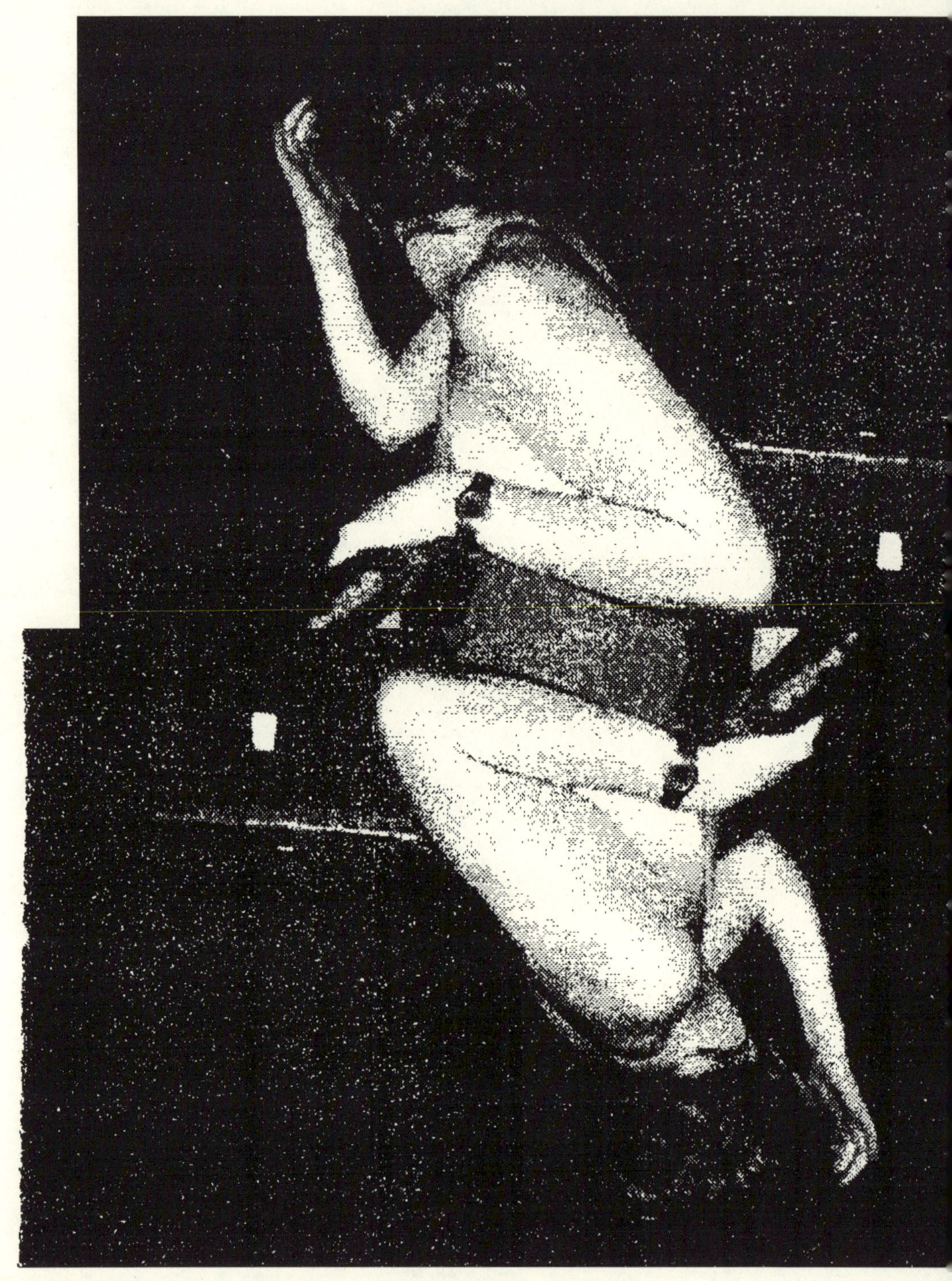

PIONEERS IN THE STUDY OF MOTION

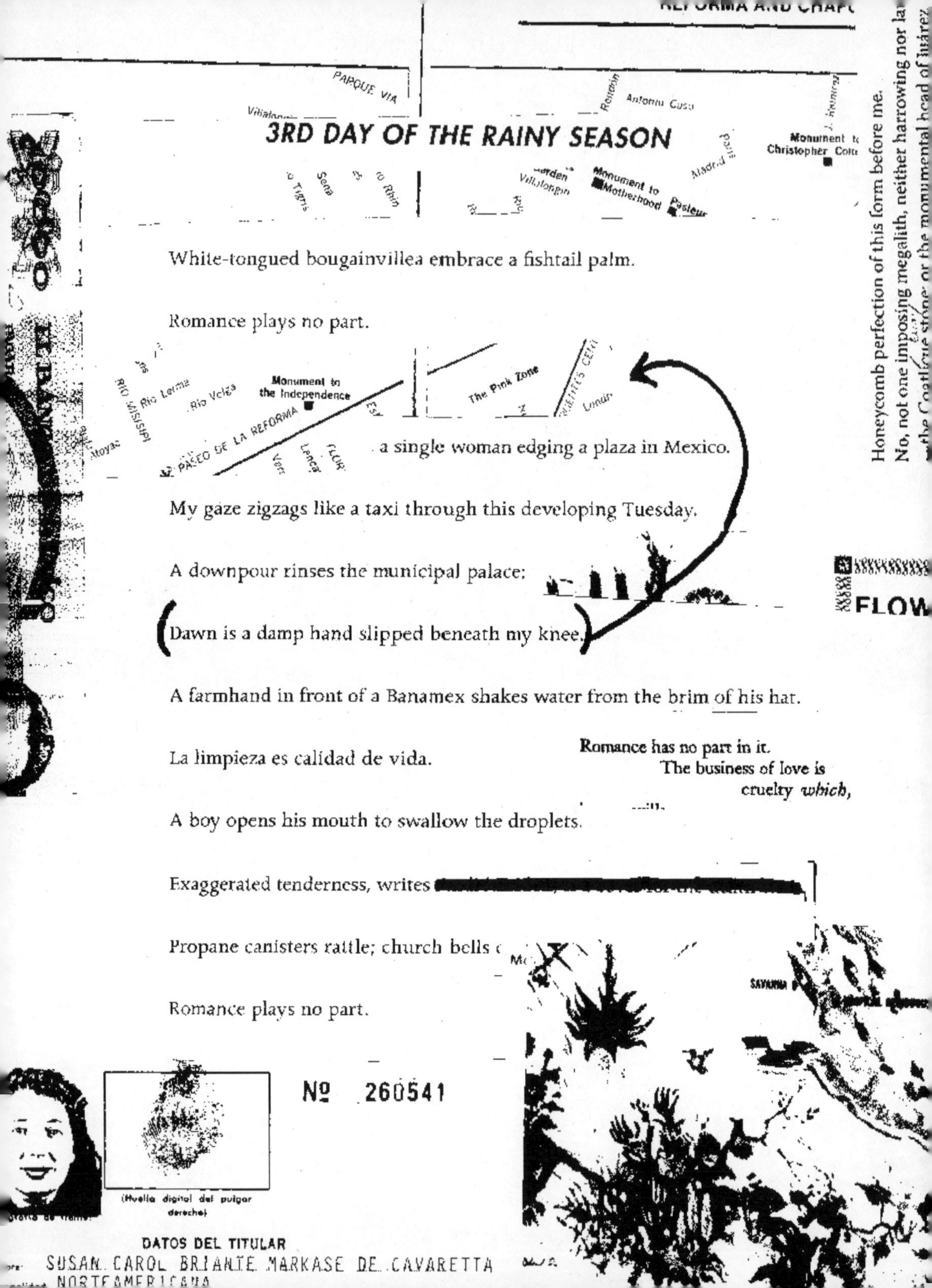

3RD DAY OF THE RAINY SEASON

White-tongued bougainvillea embrace a fishtail palm.

Romance plays no part.

a single woman edging a plaza in Mexico.

My gaze zigzags like a taxi through this developing Tuesday.

A downpour rinses the municipal palace:

(Dawn is a damp hand slipped beneath my knee.)

A farmhand in front of a Banamex shakes water from the brim of his hat.

La limpieza es calidad de vida.

A boy opens his mouth to swallow the droplets.

Exaggerated tenderness, writes

Propane canisters rattle; church bells

Romance plays no part.

Este documento faculta a su titular a permanecer en el país, en calidad de No Inmigrante
por 365 días, como NO INMIGRANTE-VISITANTE
acuerdo al artículo 42, fracción III de la Ley General de Población en vigor,
según oficio de autorización de esta Secretaría Núm. 71082
fecha 23/VI/94
Derechos pagados $ N$412.00
Recibo Oficial Núm. A 2881497341678 de fecha 14/VII/94
MEXICO, D.F., A 15 DE JULIO DE 1994
LA DIRECTORA DE REGISTRO Y ARCHIVO MIGRATORIO
Lugar y fecha de expedición
Sello
LIC. MA. GUADALUPE PEREZ MIRANDA
GGDG/LC
Firma del funcionario
Whole neighborhoods
REFORMA
CORAZON DE MEXICO
a fist a kick.
el Ejército todos los caminos a Ocosingo
emen nuevos ataques
the mountain Coming down
the needlework of rain
OF
GRASSLAND
LaJornada
Em
nada
er
gen
cia
TROPICAL EVERGREEN FOREST
"OK, so I sort of got the environs right as they were rendered around me. Here now, they just hover in place," in/stead,
inside of me,

14TH DAY OF THE RAINY SEASON

Hummingbirds hang against sky as white as lung.

A top sheet twists from a rooftop clothesline.

I shake soot from a hammock.

After nursing, Sara glows as pink as twilight.

Water pouring into a plastic bucket sounds like fingers on a drum.

I fall in love anything indigenous: smoketrees, the woman who scrubs my towels with a stone.

Selfish love, anxious love, colonial love, primarily Western love.

The power goes out with a thud.

A drum is an historical reference reinforcing nationalist sentiment.

Water murmurs through pipes.

Physical union, writes André Tridon, is probably the neutralization of two electric currents.

A statue of Emperor Cuauhtémoc falls into a slate silhouette.

Whole neighborhoods dim; Sara's baby tugs at the collar of my shirt.

Unstable love, detached love, underperforming love, neoliberal love.

40 percent of retail shopping in Mexico occurs at a Walmart owned outlet.

LOVE IN THE TIME OF NAFTA

For weeks it has been the same: the volcano spews steam without flame; the mountains stand useless; trees full of leaves and not enough sun to muster shade.

The rebels are captured on the cover of Newsweek, and nobody does anything about a waitress's salary, and the lemons getting sweeter, and the dusks ripening pink as wounds.

Driving north on the Periférico, a man looks up at a billboard and wonders about the name of the color being used to paint a rouge on Brad Pitt's lips. (Vermeil). He does not, however, notice his wife has not spoken to him for three hours.

The books she reads are getting longer. She has lost her faith in bottled water.

The coins she presses into his palm are worth exactly half of what they were yesterday.

WOOD FORMICA

You tap out footfalls of earlier birds.

Cream light blows through blinds as if to spite.

A typewriter is like a tin cup for the sightless.

Often, I gather twigs outside your window, bind them with hair.

From the parking lot, grackles will alert you.

Knot by knot, you should become enlightened.

Frequently feathers fall into the mouths of the blessed.

Frequently feathers remind you: use a coaster, hit the carriage return,

Like reaching into a sack of seed, you swerve from a blacktop view.

Chips of gunmetal paint, you type.

Can't you hear the buses cawing at the curb?

Come with me.

Come flutter, come nest, come start a new country

on a wood-grain Formica

coast, flaxen and sun-stroked, coffee-cup ringed,

ready to be wiped clean.

THE MISSIONARY'S PUPIL

Through royal palm and trumpet vine, he carves
and fucks and paves. He cultivates and fables.
Even the monkey grass recoils. Five building cranes
bow to sunset in a courtly silhouette. It is not indigo
that frightens him, not tension cables strung
from the Puente Solidaridad. Pastures of amaranth
tumble from an ample shawl of mountain. How much
damage is done in touch? In debt and obligation? Through acres
of marigolds untilled, he lays a tendril of the Pan-American.
Power lines stitch a careless trim. He traces their nervature:
                                        utility pole or crucifix?
Silver paths wither; each diesel down from Brownsville leaves
another widowed seamstress.

THE CARTOGRAPHER'S SONS

We climb up to the mountains like clouds, like christs, to wander beyond the cities. In addition to the difference in sea levels, there is the stark gap of languages. A new vocabulary writhes in the hard center of the jaw:

mirrored building, carburetor, safety pin, glue.

Much will go unwritten, read only in the pucker and slack of lips.
Many objects get named twice:

a plastic bowl,
a plastic bowl with a slender crack.

Translations swell, until the lyric is sung to the wrong woman, brown instead of black, velvet instead of cotton, some shallow veil of crepe, or not a dress at all, the water at certain times of the year like gauze, like the blurred lines of age or the lines that were forgotten the last time someone sang it, making her much less.

And where we had written Uxmal	*ruins*
And where we had written Aquiles Serdán	*mine*
And where we had written Taxco	*historic church*

Eventually, you realize that anything can be made in Mexico: wheelchairs, action figures, rice paper, lime. Eventually, you realize that for everything you are thinking, there is a word, sometimes two.

Alive in the hard center of the jaw,
you spell them the way they sound.

And where we had written Jojutla	*sugar refinery*
And where we had written Xochimilco	*floating gardens*
And where we had written La Fundición	*sulfur baths*

There was nothing
a bowl could not carry.

THE MORPHOLOGY OF THE FOLKTALE

after Vladmir Propp

The hero flies through the air

on steed; on a raptor; in the form of a falcon; on an '88 Harley-Davidson Electra Glide; on the board of a flying schooner; on her flying carpet; on the shoulders of a giant; in the carriage of the devil

He travels on the ground or over water

on the back of a horse or wolf; on the over pass; through the underbridge; in the wheel casing of a 747; in a green Volkswagen taxi with the meter whirling; a handless soldier carries a legless one; a sheepdog drags his master by the frayed collar of his linen shirt

He is led

a coyote ushers the hero through a desert; red cotton thread unwinds like a clock from his lady's hem

He makes use of stationary means of communication

he climbs a stairway; he finds a subway passage; he walks across the back of an enormous pike as if across a suspension bridge

He follows bloody tracks

to the cougar's lair; to a rusty tin; to the pulpit; to the villain; to one red flame burning above the charred door of her hermitage

EVENTUAL DARLING (MEXICO CITY)

A spire, a scalpel, a needle or the flagpole
in front of the Metropolitan Cathedral,

the horizon pitches south, demands
and remedies written out long hand on cotton sheets

bleach-scented, sweat-damp as mothers-
in-law before the National Palace sell plastic flowers

from a wrought iron fence, indiscriminate in class
or species, soldiers lower the flag in spread

and crease, to transmit infective histories
(just a twinge) the Keynesian vaccine

inspires steeples like the Pemex Tower or the Torre Latino
a fevered palm unfurls in a gesture,

in a fresco, of nation building toward me

12TH DAY OF THE RAINY SEASON

Along the Pan American Highway, farmhands wade through fields of roses.

Pills linger on the tongue like moths on water.

Droplets of pollen slip from anther to stamen.

I wait at a tollbooth with market bag and notebook.

A stem's placability should not be mistaken for delicateness.

"Breathe deep," the doctor told me and slid his stethoscope like a coin over my chest.

A seat by the window suffices to stitch the world together.

Consider the number of heartbeats per minute within this pasture of traffic.

Exaggerated mania for identification, writes André Tridon, is a symptom of weakness.

Vaya con dios. Frene con motor.

During a season of vinegary prescriptions, I sketch market bags and produce.

When fertilization takes place, ovaries swell, each petal folds like a fist.

Before a sloshing door at the back of the bus, who wouldn't resent the IMF?

Along the Pan American Highway, a beekeeper tends the blue cabinets of his hives.

A billboard celebrates: 300,000 more miles of pavement.

WHAT DOES A NON IMPERIAL LYRIC LOOK LIKE?

THE DREAM OF THE UNIFIED FIELD

I

Yes, I did know it was the money I earned as a poet that
paid
for the bombs and the planes and the tanks
that they used to massacre your family
But I am not an evil person
The people of my country aren't so bad
You can expect but so much
from those of us who have to pay taxes and watch
American TV
You see my point;
I'm sorry.
I really am sorry.

China

We live on the third world from the sun. Number three. Nobody tells us what to do.

The people who taught us to count were being very kind.

It's always time to leave.

If it rains, you either have your umbrella or you don't.

In their book *The Undercommons*, theorists Fred Moten and Stefano Harvey sketch out relationships between race, labor, speech, and exploitation.

"The compulsion to tell us how you feel," write Moten and Harvey, "is the compulsion of labor, not citizenship, exploitation not domination, and it is whiteness."

The compulsion to tell us how you feel is also a compulsion of the lyric.

THE MARKET WONDERS

When one is a woman, when one is writing poems, when one is drawn through a passion to know people today and the web in which they, suffering, find themselves, to learn the people, to dissect the web, one deals with the processes themselves. To know the processes and the machines of process: plane and dynamo, gun and dam.

— Muriel Rukeyser

An economy is a system of apparently willing but actually involuntary exchanges. A family, for example, is really a shopfront, a glass plate open to the street.

—Bhanu Kapil

TOWARD A POETICS OF THE DOW

Every day has a number attached to it. Great additions, subtractions. This is not just an aesthetic problem (see Ashbery). There is a "natural impulse toward the boundedness of closure." The bell rings, trading stops. But the world is "unfinished" (Hejinian). Both the rivers and their banks are moving. The poem remains incomplete. The trading day long over.

I do not believe if I follow the Dow I will find nirvana, but I often check the numbers, sit for meditation.

Even when we think we are at the end, there are decimals.

*

When the Buddha touched his finger to ground at the moment of enlightenment, all the leaves fell from the Bodhi tree. It is February 10, 10:04 in the morning, the Dow falls to 12194. The present poetic strives toward total awareness, incessant recording.

Ravenous as a black walnut tree, roots sucking at the sewer line, the Dow touches everything: the taste of our water, color of our sky, torque of our engines. It is February 10, 10:15 in the morning, the Dow at 12203 is rising. The poet—like the trash tree—uses all of it.

A poem moves as does the Dow influenced by a variety of factors and events: mergers, oil spills, revolutions, suffering. Sometimes what does not move tells the story. I like poems that go to prisons and coal mining towns. I like poems that act as archive or a view to Elizabeth Street. I admire circuitry and cosmology. I write with a power industry dictionary on the bookshelf behind my desk, a copy of the King James, a guide to Texas trees.

Poems should evidence some degree of control, but poets should be a little volatile. The poem is a high-risk investment, a long-term commitment. Like a big dirty city, it should make you feel

a little uncomfortable.

It is February 10, 1:11 in the afternoon, the Dow falls to 12197. The poet wants to remind the Dow that the bird has something to teach it about falling and song.

*

The theoretical physicist says, “I’ve always wanted to find the rules that governed everything.”

The theoretical physicist says, “Deep laws emerge.”

I have a friend who asks about “truth” in poetry. Whenever he does, I want to send him a valentine on musty pink paper. He lives in a mid-century modern house with mid-century modern furniture carefully culled from vintage stores and eBay. He owns an old mahogany stereo cabinet, jacked up so you can listen to an iPod through it. That’s the kind of truth in which I am interested.

Plus the silence, plus the static.

Charles Olson writes, “no event/is not penetrated, in intersection or collision with, an eternal/event.”

To which I offer this corollary: no event is not penetrated, in intersection or collision with the stock market.

I wish more poets would write about money.

*

The New York Stock Exchange began when brokers met under a buttonwood tree in 1792, the year that Blake wrote "Song of Liberty," the year Shelley was born. Charles Dow created the Dow Jones Industrial Average, representing the dollar average of 12 stocks from leading American industries, on May 26, 1896, six days after the US Supreme Court introduced the "separate but equal" doctrine.

Now corporations have the same rights as people. Why can't poems? I nominate Robert Duncan's "Poem Beginning with a Line from Pindar" for president, Frank O'Hara's "Having a Coke with You" for chairman of the Senate's foreign relations committee, Gwendolyn Brooks' "In Montgomery" for attorney general—although the House will not approve it.

Brenda Hillman explains, "Shelley wants you to visit Congress when he writes/a *violet in the crucible* & when he notes/ *imagination is enlarged by a sympathy*."

Bernadette Mayer asks us "to show and possess everything we know because having it all at once is performing a magical service for survival by the use of the mind like memory."

Blake reminds us, "For everything that lives is Holy!"

*

And there is this: When you make the poem, you can hear the swish of dollars washing down the sewer line, second by second, you can hear the stock ticker ticking away.

*

Farid rests in child's pose on the living room floor. Gianna sleeps in her crib. The Dow closes its eyes. In the park across our street, nothing blooms. Winter grass the color of a lioness. My warrior. My tree.

After the fall of Mubarak, reporters talk to tailors on Cairo streets. They broadcast video of doctors who treated the revolution's wounded. People write congratulatory notes on their lab coat sleeves. We love the look of magic marker on white cloth. But no one tells us how much money we've sent the dictator over the years. How many more receive our checks? There are bigger equations, larger alphabets, scripts from which I want to unwrite myself.

In 1994, the artist Mark Lombardi began working on a series of spindled drawings that graph relationships between business and government elites, tracing paths of financial meltdowns and mergers, shady deals and convenient bedfellows. The poem, as well, can spin webs.

The archive is wide. The poem accepts yellow leaves, guide stars, a crop failing, my milk coming in. We need the aerial photograph and microscopic slides as well as something beyond our personal viewfinders. Not a ball and chain of cause and effect, but a tendency toward pattern, implication, investigations of grief and ecstasy.

The artist Mark Lombardi worked in pencil.

The poem and the stock market welcome speculation.

*

What a drag it is to be among people who fear art because they think it mocks them. The tree is nothing but the tree. Or your mother. Or the nation. Bank of America, Merck, Pfizer. Nothing changes from generation to generation except the thing seen. Rusty backhaw, golden rain tree, 3M, Alcoa, AT&T.

We record noise, interference, outliers, error.

On February 10, the Dow closes up at 12273, poised to snap a winning streak, may fall tomorrow on Cisco. Characters ticker between us. Both the river and its banks are moving. A bird rests at the end of every winter branch plotting its own flight path.

Across the dateline, markets open.

*

October 14—The Dow Closes Up 10015

I bleed a little, peyote tea waits in the refrigerator,
a Ferris Wheel spins and spins at the fair,
after the miscarriage we search
for rings with missing stones, unmatched earrings,
sell our gold, ride the Ferris Wheel bigger
than the one in Paris,
my parents pray for us, I play Dylan's "Spanish Boots"
over and over, watch a sunroof fill with night,
like seeing a film of people I recognize
but don't really know,
Schuyler says you can't get at sunset
listing colors, between the liars' trees and shopping carts
we buy a house, cry in bed, leave
the child unnamed
pink lemon pearly blue white

We stuff steel wool
into cracks along the roof,
spray silicon in gaps,
night blackens windows,
until we feel clasped
as in "here is the church
here is the steeple,"
but our friends
stay away, 3 days
after the poet's death
his email came,
a light touch,
he wrote, he wanted
to make the room light,
we hardly have enough, cut
a hole in the kitchen wall,
you can learn about time
from brick, beam, board,
what remains unmapped
is more than we know,
whenever in doubt
win the trick, the kitchen wall
does not teach missing.
  After midnight an owl
sets the dogs barking *come out,*
come out, I am dying,
the owl shuts an eye
like the unborn,
wrapped in winter
gauze, we bring
headphones wherever
we go, we leave
the shades drawn,

window closed,
another way of killing
what gets caught
between glass and screen.

I watch weather,
monitor the troubling of trees,
a stranger comes to my door
a cloud that shouldn't be there
hangs overhead like a half-lit log,
smoldering sunset—
don't roll on me!
an R.E.M. pop song post *Reckoning*
would be the last thing
I hear, the stranger
the last thing I see,
what happened
to the lead singer
who used to sing into his hair?
      Dead,
the Buddhist would say:
we die every minute
when we open like a door to the next
      as the stranger stands at the threshold
smells of liquor
asks me to buy some magazines
from the lettered present:
December 7,
Tom Waits's birthday,
Delaware Ratifies Constitution,
"Islamic" New Year,
which sounds like a mistranslation
reminds me of how I thought I
heard you rattling the gate,
Ya'aburnee
from the Arabic,
the phrase has no equivalent,
in English
      it means bury me
because I love you so much

I do not want to live
to see your grave.

MEDITATION

In the PartyStore/PierOne/Target/Kohl's parking lot,
find a desert willow among the shopping carts,

walk around it sunwise repeating:

I am the avant-garde, I am the avant-garde, I am the avant-garde

repeating:

DIY, DIY, DIY

Imagine a chart of median family incomes
as big as the parking lot—
use it to determine where to abandon your car.

I default, I default, I default

Your mind is a blood blister rising on your thumb, a ladybug.

Among these shopping carts, you fortress,
among the plastic bags you affirm:
Lo! the light from the desert trees
does not speak in numbers, costs us nothing.
Here, as in a butterfly garden, everyone crawls before flight.

TICKER

In Revelations the angel commands John the Divine *Rise and measure*! And thus begins
a prophecy a litany of calculations 40 and 2 months 2 witnesses 200 and 3-score days

2 olive trees 2 candlesticks in a singe of data John like a physicist scavenges for God 3.5 days,
4 and 20 elders, 12 stars, for the prophets to measure is to signify and separate (we diversify,

we financial officer) as in the story of the Samurai who falsely accuses his servant Okiku
of stealing 1 of his 10 delft plates, his words spreadsheet, she inventories: 1 2 3 must be

4 5 6 mistaken 7 8 9 counts again, her master will spare her if she fucks him, an equation
she refuses, he throws her down a well   a well is a chamber of calculations, an ear

a labyrinth of bone a darkness so seldom our habitat, whence Okiku endlessly counts 1 2
my genre is trauma 3 4 an obsessive ticker 5 6 my genre falls 7 8 from office buildings 9

Okiku screams like mid-level managers in the 1930s in times of stress as before a fall or angel
or robbery at gunpoint in the back seat of a taxi we see in hyper-reality, innumerable pixels

(my god, my billfold), a national debt clock ticks off the trillions, numbers jump and flip,
the minute hand slips as a doomsday clock ticks down our fate, *arithmomania* the poet said

his mind burned with numbers, how many bricks in a wall, coins in a purse, glasses on a tray, a hook,
a burr in thought to explain why vampires stop to tally beans or seeds dropped on the ground

but a hungry child simply grabs and eats,   our ticker tells a story of national precarity,
numerical OCD, John's angel commanded *Measure!* Okiku screams, my gunman barks *Give me*

your wallet or I'll fucking kill you! to submit to another's calculations is to surrender is to default
in a taxi where I hand over my money (so Google mapped, so market crashed) not counting

THE MARKET IS A PARASITE THAT LOOKS LIKE A NEST

The Market scowls,
crosses the street against traffic,
settles, hovers over a spreadsheet
with his administrative assistant
as if it were an infant, sleeps in another bed
after 3½ years of marriage,
can only sleep on half the bed
after 43 years of marriage, sees a coffin
in a shop window, grows nostalgic
for shop windows on crowded city streets
where men made picture frames, repaired
television sets, piled tools in doorways, nursed
machines to roast and grind coffee,
operated a printing press. The Market wants
to apprentice, cannot apprentice, looks
like a nest in a tree. The Market
is a parasite that looks like a nest in a tree,
howls through the ventilation system,
hairless, blind, a newborn
calf sleeping on your chest,
the curdling Market
whose milk has come in.

The Market wonders where the soul goes,
decides that God must be ruined to make the rest of us feel whole,
remembers a trip to Mexico
when he was just out of college.
O the beggars in clown paint! O the girl he never wrote!

Jacaranda, jacaranda, jacaranda

Cheap purple leaves dirtying the sidewalks.

A street named for revolution.
A street named for insurgents.
A street named for reform.

Nights when church bells rose to Aztec temples

Like the soul?

At the hostel, she told him
a body must train to hold the light of the spirit.
They fucked listening to the Rolling Stones, burning candles.
God, the Market loved Mexico and the Rolling Stones.

Then the Market had kids and it was all profit
margin and technostructure
rollerblades for a few years,
mostly he all but forgot his legs
it must be okay to be nothing
but sight after a while
all this over here, that over there
the packing slip, the manifest
toes, arches, heels, calves
like his doctor told him, relax each muscle
against all this shimmer:
grass sequined with difference,
butterflies trembling like addicts,
in a cornfield the violet is weed.

—What does pink and yellow make?

The Market's youngest daughter asks him. *

—Orange, he says.

—What does chocolate and cookies make?

—Your favorite treat.

—What do all those numbers make, Daddy?

The Market looks up from the *Wall Street Journal*.

—The ones in your hands. The Market sighs.

Why does anyone have to make anything?

*Can you ~~imagine~~ *smell* the Market picking up ~~his~~ *your* daughter ~~from school~~ *in its teeth* dragging *parts of her body* across a ~~playground~~ *landscape* touching everything ~~he~~ it touches as if it were a screen? See how reflective the glass, how *he* is an *it* is a *we*.

The Market always feels so heavy
by the sea, weighted by a thousand
sacks of coins impossible to sort, to let
go without hemorrhage, to lighten
would be to dissolve not like an ocean
against a horizon but to sink
from continent to silt to slam
down taking walls and foundations
root systems, swing sets, whole cul-de-sacs
the Market worries he is nothing
but a pile of stones when he feels so much
inside of him slipping in and out of place
and is somehow expected to speak
from one throat.

Eight three three nine eight three three nine.
Eight three three nine eight three
three nine eight.
Three three nine eight three three
Nine eight three three nine eight three
three nine, three nine, three nine
eight three three nine eight three three nine eight
three three nine eight three three nine eight three three
—nine eight three three nine eight three three nine eight three
three nine eight.

The more I move the less I feel the baby.
I track her stillness.
And what is feeling without document?
The body is not cyborg. Winter will come
with its iron tongue
lick the year clean
reveal   wires through trees.
I know, too, there is water above us
methane below. The body endures
a sickness of proximity
awaits the ill story
of winter when I'll tell the child
yes, there were leaves.

May 15—The Dow is Closed
after James Agee

Sometimes I think there should be no writing here just my checkbook registry, envelopes of receipts, browsing history, photos uploaded, list of status updates, texts received,

the postcard of a tornado someone stuck in our gate advertising a roofing company.

Our view gets wider once we fix the gutter and awning.

And Gertrude Stein writes: "After all anybody is as their land and air is. Anybody is as the sky is high. Anybody is as there is wind or no wind there."

As a child I was forbidden to climb trees. As a child I could lose whole days, wake up in a hospital bed with a deep broad ache, pills that tasted of mint and paper. As a child I learned to connect my cursive letters, memorize multiplication tables, divide and carry what was left over.

Zeppelins floated through Stein's sky,
now we carry the Zeppelins.

The tents grow nearer; the cop inside us
pulls out his mace.

June 14—The Dow Closes Down 10192

The names of 62 birds are listed in dry erase marker
what we do and see exceeds conceptual categories

what counts as real depends upon the dry erase board
joins in a continuous loop with information technology

sympathy as feedback/dialogue
sympathy in the comment box

yellow bird (unnamed) at the feeder (likes this)
a squirrel eats pears from the tree

bluegreen dragonflies fly by the tomatoes, release
the long lag between   between thought|sentence

what at first appears to be a Graph Theory problem
is a simple Longest Common Subsequence problem

just as yesterday's seminary students with thick library books
suggest an unwillingness to invest in certain claims

to the bird I seem bigger than I am
to the sky—another matter all together (3 people like this)

i .
to make one thing of me, writes Rilke
or to "work me, Lord" as Janis sings
like a field song, mocking
-bird variations
for which I can find no equivalent, and no sooner
        have I written this down then
I want to post it on a screen where I can see all
manner of bodies burned, burdened, crushed
by the weight of factories, here stitched into this night
gown, look up from this screen, which holds all manner
of soldiers before/during/after their tours of Afghanistan,
drones, the actress
like some lesser martyr
who cuts off her breasts,
now flickering before me, cold candle, a fire
I cannot feel hums through me particle sure as any unseen
cancer or cracks in the wall of the garment factory
("work me, Lord") covered in paint

ii.
why must man always take on things
map galaxies, name particles
while factories burn, ash rises to satellites,
the question I carry around like a locket
with a dead child's hair, the question
of dead children comes
with mine
begins "the world
which is economic system does not care"
and in the wilderness beyond which is particle attraction
and distraction I slip from the grip of garment
factory fire, to ask
over and over:
          can you take it all
in, galaxy after galaxy, open your eyes sky wide
through love or force or training?

iii.
let's remember this sky
and underneath the factory workers like a thought
that dark matter thinks, a fluttering candle,
let's place ourselves beneath the hood of night
you can't gate this, razor wire, Guantanamo Bay this
the hospice nurse says rest
in the space between breaths
                    let there be space
in your gaze, let there be nurse
before you post your status update, wash
clothes, pull up the rug,
like my status update, my revolutionary status update

TICKER

In Revelations John measures the walls of New Jerusalem (144 cubits) walls fix the promised
in a promise of containment   our friend the addict says it's hard to get up in the morning,

stay clean, slide day against day, beads on an abacus, make simple calculations, in folktales
a spell like a market algorithm changes fate, a stepmother turns 11 princes into 11 swans

tells them "Fly out into the world and make your own living," their sister must spin nettles
into sweaters to break the curse,   every theory is fabric and calculation,

I measure from middle finger to elbow (15.25 in.) knee to hip (18.75 in.) any tailor
would know me better, every system binds   in Europe men raised cathedrals 144 cubits

to bring the dimensions of heaven to earth, numbers taken literally like pills (our addicts, our
prophets) or spells as in a folktale when the sister of the prince-swans is sentenced to death

for witchcraft carried to the stake before she can finish her youngest brother's sweater
she throws 11 sweaters over 11 swans who become 11 princes but one carries a swan's wing

in place of an arm, his sister becomes queen, the end is meant to be happy,   my dissertation
adviser told the story to remind us when writing: You can live with 1 arm. But can you live

on 1 income? every sweater is a series of patterns Revelations spirals in sequences 7 eyes 7 heads
7 horns 7 days to world-create, a number of completion and 3.5 that number halved, a number

unfinished, of demons, every system patterns and we learn to see at half glance
(half prince/half swan) our ancestors scoured the ground for game, nuts, berries

and when they looked up (eyes scaling a wall) they saw grains and forbs of light in the sky,
in time we counted stars, but first we drew pictures, told stories, to find our place in the night.

THE MARKET AS COMPOSITION

On February 10, 10:04 in the morning, the Dow falls to 12194. Who swims? Who rafts or islands? Rivers rise like the Southern Pacific Railroad Company. Characters ticker between us; characters leaf. Both the river and its banks are moving

past a grove of southern trees. Mimosa, magnolia, Osage orange. Our indexing makes trails through a forest of mind. Hot linked, jumpy. On the day William Carlos Williams died the Dow closed up 667. Branches

scrawl across a winter white sky. Black branch, yellow leaf. Sequined with difference. At the moment of enlightenment, when the Buddha touched his finger to the ground, all the leaves fell off the Bodhi tree. Religion

has the touch of a bird through grass. Wood duck, gadwall, northern pintail. On the day Robert Creeley died the Dow closed up 10540. The Dow closed down 1130 on the day Prince released *Purple Rain*.

You call a yellow leaf gold to stop a child's crying. Golden rain tree, rusty backhaw, sycamore, elm. A penmanship branches across sky, stiff as dialect, hard as the 14th amendment.

An eddy in a river makes a small cup of world. Hooded merganser, cooper's hawk, northern harrier. Write your headnote in the sky, like the court reporter, J. C. Bancroft Davis who wrote, *obiter dictum*, corporations have the same rights as individuals. It is sad

to be among people who don't read, who fear art because they think it mocks them. The river
is nothing but river. Or your mother. Or the nation. Merck,

Microsoft, Pfizer. Draw water, carry firewood, bear this instant. In the prolonged present, you hear dollars tick. Leaves static. Leaves distract. On the day Robert Rauschenberg died the Dow closed up 12828. Water rushes over stones with a touch as light as a court stenographer. Winter branches scribble *obiter dictum*. Nothing changes from generation to generation except the thing seen. Rusty backhaw, golden rain tree, 3M, Alcoa, AT&T. Hot linked and jumpy as the sunset over a gas station

and that makes composition, makes an index, makes a footpath out of yellow leaves.

I am no longer certain about the origin of things. My child does not sleep. So when I recalled the blond haired woman in the red dress playing a ukulele and my recognition—yes that's how you learn to play, with a humble fret board, smaller neck—I could not remember whether I had seen her on television or in a dream

nor could I find the bit in *The Autobiography of Alice B Toklas* about Picasso and Stein turning a corner in Paris to see the camouflaged tank; Picasso stammering something about it is we who have created that. His recognition before the tank was aesthetic not systemic.

But mostly I was interested in that turning

or the story about Petit Jean on a fishing boat who turns to a young Lacan and points to the glimmer of a floating sardine tin. Do you see it? He gestures to the object sparkling on the water's surface. Well, it doesn't see you.

Ten years ago when I left New York I gave up the guitar, so when I first saw the blonde-haired woman (wherever I saw her) I thought that I should have started with a smaller instrument. But as I watched more closely her intricate fingering, the finest needlepoint, I realized it was not a matter of ease but of tune.

An instrument might be a string of equations, technique, process, transaction.

I wanted to fall in love with a procedure, but I could not fall in love with a procedure because I could not always hear its song.

July 8

In the stop-start of morning, I look to take leaps, find a place to hold my daughter. Her accounting is small, and her morning is a tide that sand-shifts like traffic.

I wish we had Schuyler to meet us at the beach to add this up and turn away like gulls or waves or Olson to show us how this shift made land for our house and what's underneath before the continents splintered apart.

It's not all mind, bodies

are different where they land and what they can do this deep in a year, this far toward shore, this close to traffic and waves.

And by daughter I mean any obligation and by mother I mean any tragedy.

First there is a moment, then a poem. A man hangs a ladder from utility wires, another witnesses on his front steps—which is artist? Over the beach an airplane hauls an advertisement for a hospital.

An invisible calculus exists beyond the page, a second story leaf tremble, that view exactly with the powerline running through

I want you to see it *here* where I stop writing because my child calls to me from another room.

ADDENDUM

After my daughter stops nursing, my body continues to make milk and this spawns tender fantasies or wretched comparisons as in the last scene from *The Grapes of Wrath* when corporate farmers let peaches spoil on the branch while a young mother nurses a starving old man after her stillbirth.

Things rot. Markets make no exceptions. How many poems should I make this morning? My grandmother was a wet nurse.

While the mourning doves coo, I am reading Marx: capitalist, bourgeoisie, proletariat, aristocracy, millocracy, moneyocracy. The oligarchs roost.

After the fall of the Soviet Union, the Cuban engineer told me water was shut off for hours each afternoon. Power outages lasted for days. Neighbors gathered at battery-operated radios, networks knit around scarcity and excess. Who were those other children who nursed where my father did?

For weeks after weaning, my breasts sting. I spend the day poem counting. One book gets you a job, two get you tenure. The poem machine turns factory.

The mourning doves aren't talking like it is 30 years ago, aren't talking like a family could live on one income.

When I was a child, the engineer told me, the revolution was the most beautiful thing. *La cosa más bella*. Then the engineer went hungry. Some critics claim Steinbeck's dying old man is capitalism is communism is our twentieth century Pietà.

Lack something long enough, and a market springs up like a peach tree straining toward the sun. Even the mourning doves know this—the lesson of the nest is improvisation.

TICKER

A pattern imposes form on cloth and on the fingers of a teenage girl under factory light
who picks, spins, measures, a circuit behind a screen, brand on a body, current routed,

stitched across countries: 42 months 1,260 days, 2 olive trees, 2 lampstands, .27 of US households live
in "asset poverty" without savings to cover 3 months of expenses, an auspicious number, a laptop

powers up, everything patterns: 12 stars, 7 heads, 10 horns, 7 crowns and outside the Green
Zone of our 1st-world economy 3.5 days, .1 of the city, 7,000 people, 2nd woe, 3rd woe,

7th angel, a rose moans through prickly pear, thorn loves thorn, in drought, a petal
falls to shrapnel, the desert light trains us to love the pallid   survival flaunts

like a national soccer team, whatever is weak welcomes,   John was exiled
to Patmos, his story spirals in repetitions, extends a fabric of waves and particles and string,

a portfolio of catastrophe that spins round like Blake, Ginsberg, Kocot, McSweeney,
I never read biographies of famous poets because they make me anxious about money

measuring signifies and contains, of the 7 beatitudes in Revelations the first begins *Blessed*
is he who reads: folktale, verse, portfolio, spreadsheet, the American dream is fairytale:

say you want to ghost, say you want to go rogue from this set of data,   there is no
cloud, no cover, I don't walk much lately but I know exactly what streets hoard the shade,

between a shadow and myself   a theory, an exchange, my husband's Facebook status asks:
"You know you are middle class when ___________"

there is a way/no way to be absent from the system.   *Unsubscribe, Unsubscribe, Unsubscribe,*
I put some of my life, my love, in a space between numbers, between the values

against which they are judged, I have set a ticker (tick, tick, tick,) like Muriel Rukeyser does
in "The Book of the Dead"   numbers kill and crowd, dive and ascend stick like nettles

like burrs on my skirt sewn by some teenage girls in a foreign country with only the language
of numbers, between us   my numerical vision makes me: prophet, addict, lonely,

my genre is national hunger a trauma narrative repeats, the lesson of the nest
is scavenge and weave, as ocotillo points to a place where clouds used to be.

MOTHER IS MARXIST

My daughter plays hide and seek with the white floor-length panel curtains in front of our living room window. Dusk traffics light, the sunset scans her. She is gold leafed wrapped in the curtain before the window.

Can't you see her gold?

*

"I do not know whether you have seen the building of the Metropolitan Company in New York. ..." Charles Coolidge Read stated before the Massachusetts Legislature in 1895. "Go up to the directors' room where the floor is soft with velvet carpets and the room is finished in rich red mahogany there you will find these gentlemen who think what a beautiful thing this child insurance is ... "

Read insisted that from every block of marble in the Metropolitan Company building peered "the hungry eyes of some starving child."

In 1895, one could purchase a $10 life insurance policy for a one-year-old child or a $33 policy for a 10-year-old child for 3 cents a week. One and a half million children were insured in the United States in 1896. By 1902, that number climbed to over 3 million.

Advocates said the policies served as funerary insurance as well as protected poor and working class families against a loss of income at a time when child labor was common. Opponents, like Read, believed it provided incentive for poor or working class parents to neglect or outright murder their children for profit. Such opponents never questioned the ease with which they believed poor or working class parents might be tempted to kill their children. Actual incidents of infanticide related to child insurance appear to be rare.

Still, a writer for the *Boston Evening Transcript* declared: "No manly man and no womanly woman should be ready to say that their infants have pecuniary value."

*

When we lived in the two-bedroom house on a busy street on the fringes of a "good" neighborhood in Dallas, once every a couple of months I would hear gunshots, often on Saturday nights, usually late enough that I was in bed.

We purchased the house through the Obama tax credit program for first-time homebuyers, a response to the economic crisis of 2008 and the housing market crash. Because we could not afford to put 20 percent down, we had two mortgages, the second of which included a balloon payment.

We purchased the two-bedroom house on a busy street on the fringes of a "good" neighborhood in Dallas because we were trying to have a baby and the neighborhood had the best public elementary school as well as two Montessori charter schools.

*

The average per student expenditure for public elementary and secondary schools in 2012–13 ranged from a high in Vermont of $19,752 per student to a low in Arizona of $6,949. In FY 2022, average per student expenditure for public schools widened from a high of $29,873 in New York to $9,552 in Utah.

*

The market scans my child, calculates pecuniary value.

Parents register and respond often seeking out places (the "good" neighborhood or private school) where a child's value is high enough in relation to the needs of others to make them relatively safe

or a parent may reaffirm existing market valuations.

And if the child is female or presents as female
And if the child is queer or presents as queer
And if the child is poor or presents as poor
And if the child is of color or ethnic or presents as of color or ethnic

a little spark of mica in a field

of sand.

*

Pregnant women and new mothers have a heightened sense of smell and easily disrupted pattern of sleep.

*

One night after a particularly loud series of gunshots heard from the bedroom of our two-bedroom house on a busy street on the fringes of a "good" neighborhood in Dallas, Farid called the police. I don't remember what he said, what kind of injury we could have reported, what response we expected.

When we bought the house, we joined the neighborhood association. We also had the option of paying an additional $180 for "an off-duty police officer to patrol our neighborhood each week" as well as "answer our emails" and provide "special patrols" while we were away.

Per day, per pupil, per square foot

many parents may want to register and respond to the values the market places on their child, but a parent's own depressed value may leave her with scant time to challenge market valuations of her children, child, self.

"Boys are easier to raise than girls," my mother told me.

I feel my depressed value as a woman
as well as my surplus value as a white ethnic.

The consultant in the TED talk teaches me to stand bigger.

*

In 1908 a ten-year-old girl working in a mill made 30 cents a day.

In 1911 an eight-year-old girl shucking oysters made 30 cents to 35 cents a day.

An eight-year-old boy, who had been shucking for three years, earned 45 cents a day.

In 1917 a ten-year-old girl working on a tobacco farm made 50 cents a day.

As recently as 2014 the Human Rights Watch reported it remained "perfectly legal" in the United States "for a 12-year-old to work 50 or 60 hours a week in tobacco fields, as long his or her parents' consent and the work doesn't directly conflict with school hours." In 2024, Alabama, Indiana, Iowa, Kentucky and West Virginia all enacted legislation to weaken childhood labor protections.

*

Often the day after hearing gunfire from my bedroom of our two-bedroom house on a busy street on the fringes of a "good" neighborhood in Dallas, I would scan the internet looking for some piece of news to link to the sounds. I never found mention of a shootout or injury or killing.

The gunshots existed as fragments in a storyline that seemed to have no relation to me, a non sequitur, a piece of conversation overheard in a language in which I had no fluency.

But those metaphors are wrong.

My legislative representatives cannot or will not pass gun control policy, my tax dollars support the purchase of surplus military equipment by police. The white imaginary criminalizes non-white bodies.

*

From 2001–2011, Department of Homeland Security grants provided police departments with $34 billion to fund their militarization, making profits for military contractors and for-profit law enforcement training organizations

like special ops supplier Blackhawk Industries (founded by a former Navy SEAL), ThunderSledge breaching tools, Lenco Armored Vehicles bulletproof box trucks, KDH Defense Systems's body armor, like HaloDrop "flying robotic services for serious incidents and situations," D-Co, Leaders and Training LLC, like Innovative Tactical Training Solutions, like Winchester Ammunition.

Every altercation helps justify the militarization of police

and someone makes money makes money makes money makes money.

*

I want to teach my child to shed numbers like a skin in the summer, in the shimmering heat of the ever-warming summer.

*

We were able to afford the two-bedroom house on the fringes of a "good" neighborhood in Dallas because it sat on a street with six lanes of traffic separated down the middle by a small park or a large median of trees.

Most of the windows in the house were painted shut. Many rattled from the vibration of passing cars.

We kept a small padlock on the gate at the top of our driveway.

Before the padlock, men sometimes came to our door smelling of liquor selling magazines or asking to use our phone. Once I watched an old sedan lurch onto the sidewalk in front of our house. A woman shouted from the driver's seat while a man reluctantly exited from the passenger side, pieces of clothing flying out the door and window after him.

From the front windows of the house you could see cottonwoods, oaks, and black walnut trees. From almost anywhere in the house you could hear the traffic.

*

Mothers attempt to erase the integers, to move decimals, to point out discrepancies in the ledger, disrupt the protocols of exchange.

When the mothers of the victims of police violence march on Washington, DC,

when mothers in Central America set their children like paper lanterns

on a breeze,

when warehouses of children wait at our border,

Mother is Marxist, exposing as false and pernicious the mystification of capitalist instantiations of value, promiscuous relations of value and their violence.

Mother is not a biological or relational subject position but can be an attitude of resistance before the market.

*

Underfunded public schools show their cinder block, reveal their district paint purchased from the lowest bidder, can't hide their too many desks, their too tired, their underpaid.

You see it in their lunch trays.

Private schools flaunt their walls of windows, famous architect library, flagstone pathways, full-time counselor.

In such places, children learn to read their market value.

*

Scholar Viviana A. Zelizer explains: "Children's insurance began as outright bets among 16th-century European businessmen on the birth and lives of boys and girls."

*

A police officer flaunts his gun and in the amount of time your child is afforded to pull their hand from their pocket

you can learn their market value.

*

Value differentiates. Metaphor makes false equations.

When we talk about metaphor we talk about "vehicles," but metaphor can erase distance, conceal the mode of transport: the ride hiding in the wheel well of the 747 or the journey along a dry riverbed through the Sonoran night.

*

The work of all mothers is not equal, although the goal to challenge market valuations may be the same. The market exploits our attachments, makes its violent calculations. The market, mothers, divides and divides us.

And someone makes money makes money makes money makes money.

I want to slur the calculations.

*

My love for my daughter is dumb and simple
all of my feeling focused, funneled
into the leaky sewer line
running down our front yard of our two-bedroom house
from which the black walnut trees feed.

*

Sentimentality is a shard from the shop front window of family. What sliver of American plate glass do you see?

I sympathize with the desire to throw a brick through a shop window and steal a television set.

But sympathy is never enough.

*

Children are not paper lanterns set on a breeze.

Imagine cutting off an arm to save the body.

*

Dear mother, you feel like the arm

*

In Tucson, we buy a 2–2 house in a "good neighborhood" with a neighborhood association. We no longer hear gunshots at night. We no longer have the chance to pay for additional police patrols or attention. We hope to get our daughter into a better elementary school than the one in our neighborhood through an open enrollment lottery.

Often we fall asleep to the sound of helicopters or planes taking off or landing at the nearby Davis-Monthan Air Force Base: the A-10 Thunderbolt II or the HH-60G Pave Hawk helicopter, the HC-130J Combat King II transport, the F-16C or F-16D Fighting Falcon.

In the pre-Tr*mp era, when I originally wrote this (circa 2014) the financial advisory giant Deloitte predicted continued decline in revenue for the global defense sector, with the US defense budget "a key driver of this decline." Still Deloitte gave A+ ratings to stocks in this sector including Textron, Honeywell, Huntington, and Curtiss-Wright.

In 2024, the *Breaking Defense* newsletter explained that global defense revenues grew in 2023. In November 2024, *Forbes* reported shares for the multibillion dollar private prison companies Core Civic and GeoGroup increased value by 75 percent and 76 percent respectively since Election Day.

*

Unmanned aerial vehicles, better known as drones, scan the Sonoran Desert for moving bodies.

There are no accurate numbers for the children killed by US drones outside of our country.

Sometimes when I look up I can see the pale underbelly of the HC-130J Combat King II transport gliding over the streets of my neighborhood or the playground of my daughter's preschool like a hand passing over a velvet rug in the board room of an insurance company.

*

If we traveled far enough, we could find 1,000 children waiting on the border, they were walking toward us.

WHAT DOES AN ANTICAPITALIST POEM LOOK LIKE?

"Real" poems do not "really" require words.

Layli Long Soldier, "38"

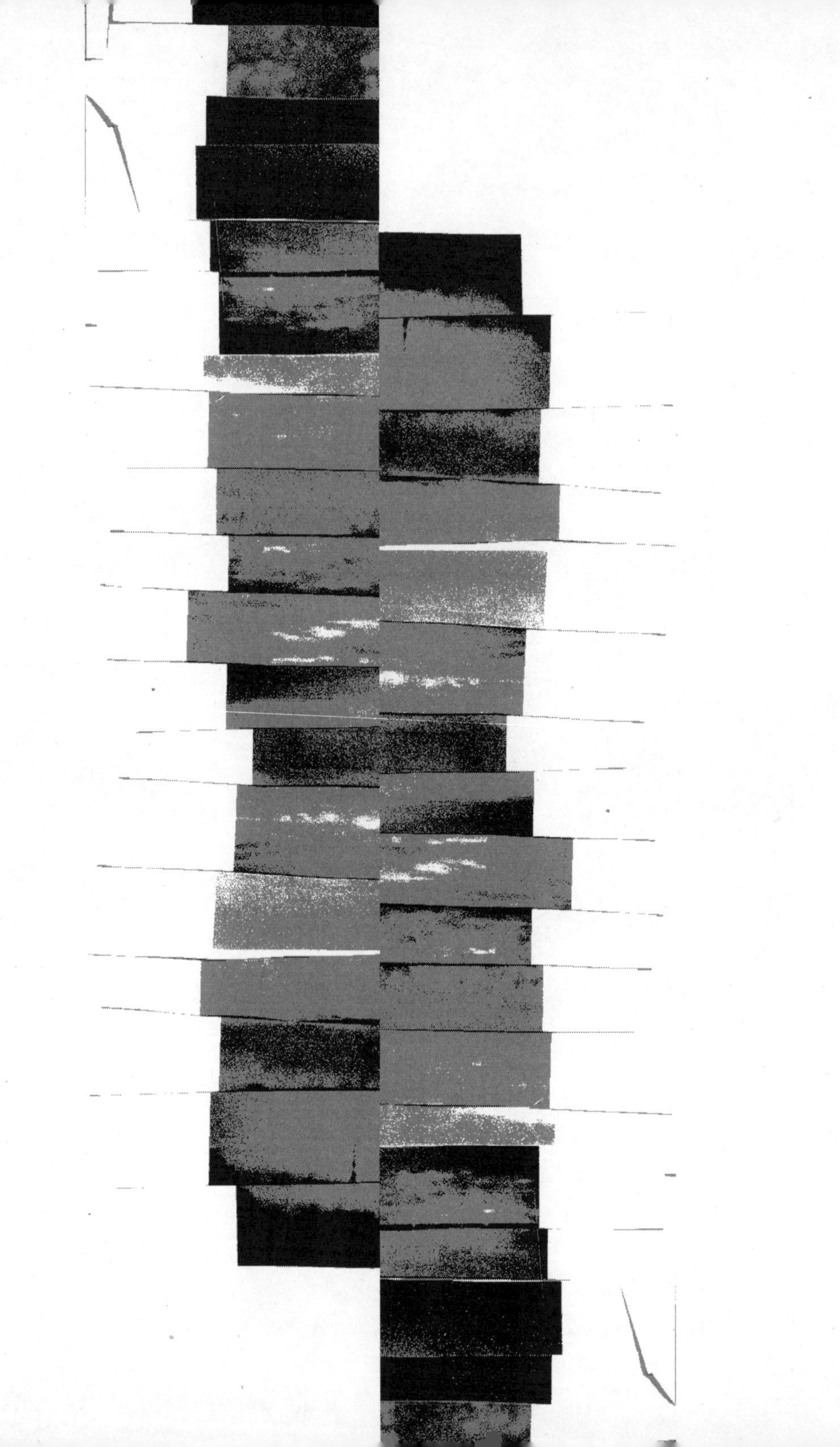

DEFACING THE MONUMENT

Why don't ya have it all

Yes a little

BEFORE HONORABLE ERIC J. MARKOVICH
OPERATION STREAMLINE
SPECIAL PROCEEDINGS COURTROOM - 2nd FLOOR
Tuesday, September 26, 2017

he is very nervous

COURTESY DRAFT COPY

17-27739MP [redacted] 8 USC 1325(a)(1) ILLEGAL ENTRY

DOA: 09/24/2017

ATTY Rodolfo Valenzuela (CJA)

TRUE NAME: Speaks English: No

Thinking clearly today – si
Are u pleading guilty vol + of you own free will
pause si
no shackles

17-27741MP [redacted] 9/24 - Nogales 8 USC 1325(a)(1) ILLEGAL ENTRY 6 months

DOA: 09/24/2017

ATTY Micaela Portillo (CJA)

TRUE NAME: Speaks English: No

think clear + are you pleading guilty – Yes
has anyone promised you anything to get you to plead guilty
do you under the offense – yes

17-27742MP [redacted] 8 USC 1325(a)(1) ILLEGAL ENTRY

DOA: 09/25/2017

ATTY Raymond Panzarella (CJA)

TRUE NAME: Speaks English: No

yes – clear head
yes – volun + of yr own free will
do you under the offense – yes – do you under consequences – yes

17-27743MP [redacted] ✓ 8 USC 1325(a)(1) ILLEGAL ENTRY

DOA: 09/25/2017

ATTY Joe Machado (CJA)

TRUE NAME: Speaks English: No

9/23
Lukeville w/o port of entry
guilty

17-27744MP [redacted] 8 USC 1325(a)(1) ILLEGAL ENTRY

DOA: 09/25/2017

ATTY Vincent Lacsamana (CJA)

TRUE NAME: Speaks English: No

17-27748MP [redacted] 8 USC 1325(a)(1) ILLEGAL ENTRY

DOA: 09/25/2017

ATTY Thomas Jacobs (CJA)

TRUE NAME: Speaks English: No

17-27750MP [redacted] * 8 USC 1325(a)(1) ILLEGAL ENTRY

DOA: 09/25/2017

ATTY Alfred Islas (CJA)

TRUE NAME: Speaks English: No

9/22
Sasabe
yes
guilty

Short blue shirt

4 microphones

Did you enter the US w/ immig doc or did you walk through the desert?

The word "economic" does not appear in the text of the Deparment of Homeland Security's webpage entitled "Obtaining Asylum in the United States,"

is not uttered into the court record.

The word "economic" remains in my mouth at the back of the courtroom, where I sit scribbling on a legal pad, trying to trace a relation to the seven men who stand before the judge shackled at the wrists, waists, and ankles.

The body is a condition–the nation another.

I used to believe the document tethered the poem to the earth, to soil that one could taste, that could be nutrient to more than one.

But a document can pull a nation out from under you.

In the US District Court, Arizona District, shackles chime like the rigging of a ship in harbor in the moments before a voyage. Seven men approach the bench, one by one they speak directly into the microphone

to become a name in a document, a few words in the record, and one syllable of consent.

Do you understand the rights that you are giving up, the consequences of pleading guilty and the terms of your written plea agreement? Are you pleading guilty voluntarily and of your own free will? Are you a citizen of the United States? On or about March 17, 2017, did you enter the United States from Mexico near Nogales without coming through a designated port of entry? How do you plead to the charge of illegal entry?

Do you understand the rights that you are giving up, the consequences of pleading guilty and the terms of your written plea agreement? Are you pleading guilty voluntarily and of your own free will? Are you a citizen of the United States? On or about March 18, 2017, did you enter the United States from Mexico near Lukeville without coming through a designated port of entry? How do you plead to the charge of illegal entry?

Do you understand the rights that you are giving up, the consequences of pleading guilty and the terms of your written plea agreement? Are you pleading guilty voluntarily and of your own free will? Are you a citizen of the United States? On or about March 14, 2017, did you enter the United States from Mexico near Sasabe without coming through a designated port of entry? How do you plead to the charge of illegal entry?

Do you understand the rights that you are giving up, the consequences of pleading guilty and the terms of your written plea agreement? Are you pleading guilty voluntarily and of your own free will? Are you a citizen of the United States? On or about March 18, 2017, did you enter the United States from Mexico near Nogales without coming through a designated port of entry? How do you plead to the charge of illegal entry?

Do you understand the rights that you are giving up, the consequences of pleading guilty and the terms of your written plea agreement? Are you pleading guilty voluntarily and of your own free will? Are you a citizen of the United States? On or about March 15, 2017, did you enter the United States from Mexico near Sasabe without coming through a designated port of entry? How do you plead to the charge of illegal entry?

In 2005, Operation Streamline began the prosecution of unauthorized migrants, often sending them to prison prior to deportation. Each migrant leaves the proceedings with a criminal record.

In this sense, the process is documentary. Immigration rights advocates have called the proceedings "assembly line justice," because as many as 75 migrants might be brought before a judge in a single day, plead guilty to the felony offense of unauthorized entry or re-entry into the United States to serve jail time or face jail time should they be caught again.

Proponents call the process a "deterrent" despite evidence that most of those caught will try to cross again. Many have family in the United States and have lived here for years prior to deportation. Others flee violence or death threats. Others flee desperate economic conditions. The threat of criminal prosecution and imprisonment often compels those attempting to cross to do so in remote and dangerous terrain, increasing the risk of suffering and death, allowing our immigration policy to turn the desert into a weapon. Since Operation Streamline was first introduced, the border death rate has risen 127 percent from 52 deaths per 100,000 apprehensions to 118 deaths per 100,000 apprehensions in 2010.

However, it is undeniable that the proceedings are successful in their goal: they turn migrants into criminals. Despite the consultations with lawyers (whom the migrants meet for the first time briefly before their hearing), despite the headsets and the court interpreter, despite the judge's (sometimes) detailed statements about rights that they are giving up in order to accept the plea bargain, some migrants do not follow what is happening.

"Do you understand the consequences of pleading guilty?" the judge asks.

"Yes, I am guilty," the migrant says.

And when the judge asks the migrant why he does not understand the question, the indigenous migrant (for whom Spanish is a second language) explains: "It's too fast."

If a line is a dot that went for a walk, then a wall is a line that divides

Nogales, Arizona, from Nogales, Sonora.

A deportee is a man who left his kids at a bus stop, was pulled over by the cops, could not produce a Social Security number and was sent first to jail, then to Nogales, Sonora, to be handed his belongings in a large ziplock bag from the Department of Homeland Security.

A frame of words can determine what one sees:

a man walks across the US-Mexico border along a partitioned walkway, a man walks across the US-Mexico border in a caged walkway, US officials escort a man across the US-Mexico border in a human cage.

And if I refer to him as a father of two.
And if I refer to him as a man.
And if I refer to him as a refugee.
And if I refer to him as a migrant.
And if I refer to him as undocumented.
And if I refer to him as a defendant.
And if I refer to him as illegal.
And if I refer to him as a criminal.

Metaphors make circles of our lives: a Venn diagram of contrast and resemblance.

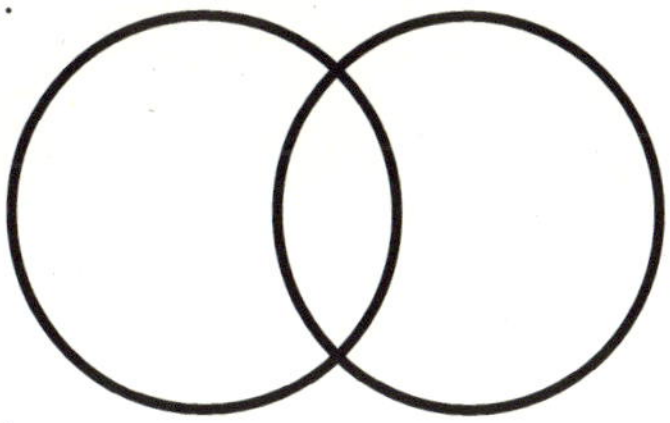

Who goes where?

In the fifth-floor apartment that serves as a migrant women and children's shelter in Nogales, Sonora: an 18-year-old girl who wants to see her father, a woman from Central America who left under death threat, a mother who fled an abusive relationship and now needs to make more money to support her children and grandchildren, and an 80-year-old who wants to cross into Nogales, AZ, for the eighth time so she can sell *paletas* from a pushcart.

A nun prods them into telling their stories to us: four women and one man visiting from a creative writing program at a state university just an hour north of them through an initiative that aims to use literary and documentary arts to diversify the stories about and expand dialogue on issues related to the border.

The eldest woman stands raising her hand as if testifying or praying. She says when the first President Bush came into office, he tried to make life hard for migrants. But we rose up, she explains, and stopped him. She says as soon as she can, she will go back to the popsicle factory, to her boss. She tells us her boss's name and address, says her boss will give her a card to help her stay

as soon as she can get back.

And the woman who fled her country under death threat says: "We want peace." Decades of US policies and interventions in Central America that favor business interests over the majority of the population, that export gang members and failed anti-gang policies, must feel like a long, dirty war.

"Do you feel better when you tell these stories?" one of us asks.

And the woman does not answer, just keeps telling her story.

"We are teaching them to make earrings," the nun explains as she brings us into another room and shows us beaded jewelry: row upon row, each piece a little memorial to every woman who has come through the shelter.

What did the nun tell them about our presence or what we might be able to do for them? Were they told we could help? Were they told we could help before the end of their two-week stay at the woman's shelter after which they would have to find their way north or back from where they came? Were they told some faulty equation of voice and change, some scrawl of hope like the flight of sparrows, stalling and diving without knowing whose house they alight upon?

What did we think we could do? Every summer for the past three I have gone to Nogales, Mexico, with students from the University of Arizona's Southwest Field Studies in Writing Program to witness and write about migration and environment issues unique to southern Arizona. And each summer, as we bear witness to conditions migrants face, we wonder: **How can we amplify voices without turning other people's stories into commodities, without re-affirming the faulty myth of "giving voice"?** We do not want to reduce the struggles of the migrants we meet to mere human interest stories. We know that writing will not be enough.

The change necessary to improve the migrant women's lives feels utterly available and beyond any single transaction.

"We will work hard," the women tell us.

"Do you have bracelets?" we eventually ask.

—

The words "economic," "family," and "asylum" remain unspoken as I sit in the back of the courtroom scribbling on a legal pad, trying to structure a context and trace my relation to the seven men who stand before the judge shackled at the wrists, waists, and ankles.

Reader, can you improvise your relation to the phrase "illegal entry," to the large seal of US District Court, District of Arizona, that hangs above the judge, eagle suspended with talons and arrows pointing?

Perhaps your relation stretches like a wall, bends like footprints toward a road, perhaps your relation spindles and barbs, chollas or ocotillos, twists like a razor wire on top of a fence.

Perhaps you do not improvise, perhaps you shackle, you type, you translate, you prosecute, you daily wage, your mouth goes dry when you speak–paper, palimpsests of silence, palimpsests of complicity and connection never made evident on the page.

Write down everything you need. How long is the list?
Sleep with it beneath your head, eat it, wear it.
Can you use it to make a little shade from an unrelenting gaze?

Speak into the court record the amount of profit extracted from such men as those before the judge shackled at the wrists, waists, and ankles not limited to the amount of profit that will be extracted from such bodies through the payments that will be made per prisoner per day to the Corrections Corporation of America and GEO Group, but also inclusive of all the profits generated by trade agreements that makes labor in the so-called developing countries so cheap.

How can we digest it?

"Best of luck to you," the judge says.

"Que le vaya bien," the lawyers say as the migrants begin their slow procession out of the courtroom in chains.

And in that moment, from the back of the courtroom,
we can decide to accept or forget what we have seen, to bear it,
or to change it

because we love it, we want it, we don't care enough to stop it,
we hate it,

we can't imagine how to stop it, we can't imagine it,
we can't imagine.

Yes a little

BEFORE HONORABLE ERIC J. MARKOVICH
OPERATION STREAMLINE
SPECIAL PROCEEDINGS COURTROOM - 2nd FLOOR
Tuesday, September 26, 2017

he is very nervous

COURTESY DRAFT COPY

17-27739MP — 8 USC 1325(a)(1) ILLEGAL ENTRY
DOA: 09/24/2017
ATTY Rodolfo Valenzuela (CJA)
TRUE NAME: — Speaks English: No

Thinking clearly today – si
Are ... guilty vol + of your own free will
pause si
no shackles

People For the American Way

Trump's America: For-Profit Prisons, Immigrant Detention and Shady Political Donations

17-27741MP — 8 USC 1325(a)(1) ILLEGAL ENTRY
DOA: 09/24/2017
ATTY Micaela Portillo (CJA)
TRUE NAME: — Speaks English: No

6 months

think clear + are you
pleading guilty – yes
has anyone promised you anything to get you to plead guilty
do you under the offense – yes

Rio Tazewell <http://www.pfaw.org/spokespeople/rio-tazewell/> April 19, 2017

NEWS AND ANALYSIS

17-27742MP — 8 USC 1325(a)(1) ILLEGAL ENTRY
DOA: 09/25/2017
ATTY Raymond Panzarella (CJA)
TRUE NAME: — Speaks English: No

yes – clear head
do you under consequences – yes

17-27743MP — 8 USC 1325(a)(1) ILLEGAL ENTRY
DOA: 09/25/2017
ATTY
TRUE NAME: — Speaks English: No

17-27744MP — 8 USC 1325(a)(1) ILLEGAL ENTRY
DOA: 09/25/2017
ATTY
TRUE NAME: — Speaks English: No

17-27748MP — 8 USC 1325(a)(1) ILLEGAL ENTRY
DOA: 09/25/2017
ATTY
TRUE NAME: — Speaks English: No

17-27750MP * — 8 USC 1325(a)(1) ILLEGAL ENTRY
DOA: 09/25/2017
ATTY Alfred Iglesias (CJA)
TRUE NAME: — Speaks English: No

The Trump administration recently awarded a $110 million contract <https://www.usnews.com/news/best-states/texas/articles/2017/04/13/texas-getting-first-immigrant-lockup-built-under-trump> to the GEO Group, one of the country's largest private prison contractors, to develop and operate a new detention facility in Texas.

9/22 sabe
injury

Short blue shirt

4 microphones

Did you enter the US w/ immig doc or did you walk through the desert?

FURTHER EXERCISES

Write a 12-line rhythmically charged poem in which you slant rhyme (at least twice) the name of the last official indicted from the Tr*mp administration. Reference the most recent climate change related disaster. Address by first name one of the 24 migrants who have died in ICE custody since 2017. End with the instructions given to you by a parent or guardian on what you should do when waking from a nightmare.

IIII

Write a poem as an acrostic of the name of a person you love who is most vulnerable to US government policies. Include a quote (unattributed) from a writer killed by an authoritarian regime or a line in which you complete the phrase:

"I have birthed ______________ and buried ______________"

End with a line that snaps like a turnstile at your back, that closes like an iron gate behind you.

IIII

Typographically represent the 650 miles of border wall teetering on the 2,000-mile US-Mexico boundary. Write a 3-word refrain that could be used as a chant to tear the shroud of normalcy. Answer the question: What brought your parents to the place they birthed you? End with a line so open it would allow both a child and an endangered Mexican gray wolf to step through.

IIII

Begin with the city from which you write. Use your five senses to describe the most recently gentrified neighborhood. Personify a "For Sale" sign or an underfunded public school. Do not include an image of a unhoused person.

IIII

Write a 48-line poem in which each line ends with you claiming "executive privilege" or some variation of that phrase. Answer the question: What do you call someone who cannot speak and comes without a name? Reference the last time you were terrified by a cop.

End with a metaphor that gasps for air or water

or end with a couplet that screeches like a line drawn in the dirt.

IIII

Write a poem that binds you and your reader as tightly as the zip ties encircling protestors' wrists. Use empathy, compassion, complicity. Include the all reasons why you have not placed your body in the streets or the courts to protect the person you love who is most vulnerable to the state. Address that person. End with a line that moans like gas entering your tank or end with a line that divides nothing.

IIII

In couplets, describe the opening shot of a movie you would make to depict the events of the past year. Slant rhyme the name of at least one known Russian hacking virus. Describe a monument, then deface it.

End by completing the phrase:

I would ____________ 2,000 miles to end ____________.

IIII

Write a poem that records all the new developments that have occurred in our country's continued assault on migrants and/or other nonwhite bodies while you were writing any one of the above poems.

IIII

Make a list of words that sound like shots being fired on a residential street or that sound like children being herded into cages. Create a poem around these words. It should not rhyme.

WHAT DOES A TWENTY-FIRST CENTURY LYRIC LOOK LIKE?

[insert yours here]

In Spring 2024 amidst the blossoming of protests, a group of Emory University students raised tents to call for an end to the Palestinian genocide and an end to the construction of the "Atlanta Public Training Center," dubbed "Cop City." They also created a document, "Emory is Everywhere," which begins:

> As the Palestine Solidarity movement rips across college campuses, college administrators and government bureaucrats are rushing to denounce anyone taking action as an "outside agitator." Those who grease the gears of the war machine think that this rhetoric will erode public support for bold actions at Emory. They are wrong.
>
> 45 years after the Camp David Accords – an infamously botched, imperialist plan for peace between Israel and Egypt with no input from Palestinians – was orchestrated by an Emory faculty alum President Carter, we observe that there is nowhere on Earth "outside" of Emory University.

The manifesto continues to implicate the institution:

> Emory University has the highest tuition, the lowest acceptance rate, and by far the highest endowment of any institution in Georgia. Economic barriers, infamously racist standardized testing, and nepotism have barred many from studying at Emory. To students in Atlanta and beyond – we invite you to struggle with us...
>
> Emory's $11 billion endowment, the 11th highest in the country, is an outsized influence in Atlanta's economy. While economic inequality widens in the city, Emory remains a bastion of the rich. To the restaurant workers, house cleaners, gig workers, and all proletarians – we invite you to struggle with us....
>
> In 2020, Emory University laid off or furloughed over 1500 employees. To those who are no longer affiliated with the university – we invite you to struggle with us...

I am not interested in this document because I harbor any particular animosity toward Emory University, another corporatized institution of higher learning, not unlike the one for which I work. The gesture in "Emory is Everywhere" that levels blame at the institution feels less important to me than the invitation it becomes. The manifesto's authors open their encampment and struggle to other students, the working class, the unemployed, and the unhoused. Their observation that "there is nowhere on Earth 'outside' of Emory University" strikes me as a rebuttal of the "we're-the-center-of-the-universe" egocentrism often used to dismiss the views of college students. Instead of sounding like the earliest astronomers, who thought the cosmos spun around the earth, the authors of "Emory is Everywhere" echo contemporary physicists who posit that the far-flung universe and every particle within it are bound by webs of strings, a weft of dark matter, and "spooky" attractions, unseen and largely inexplicable connections, between the atomic particles that make up ourselves and our world.

*

In January 1971, Fannie Lou Hamer addressed a predominantly white audience at the University of Wisconsin in Madison to raise money for her Freedom Farm Co-op, which grew food for the poor in her home state of Mississippi. Nixon was just a year in office and a little less than three years from impeachment. The Vietnam War continued to rage. Hamer, a former sharecropper, founded the Mississippi Freedom Democratic Party, spoke at the 1964 Democratic National Convention, and organized the Freedom Summer, bringing hundreds of college students, Black and white, to register African American voters in the segregated South.

During her speech, she reminded her Wisconsin crowd of the work of other white Civil Rights activists, Michael Schwerner and Andrew Goldman, brutally murdered in Mississippi by Ku Klux Klan members in 1964 along with James Chaney. She told the white audience: "And when they died, they didn't just die for me, but they died for you because your freedom is shackled in chains to mine. And until I am free, you are not free either."

Hamer continued: "And if you think you are free, you drive down to Mississippi with your Wisconsin license plate, and you will see what I am talking about."

No where is outside Mississippi, she might have said.

*

In the wake of the election to the US presidency of a convicted criminal, who tried to overturn the results of a previous presidential election and who seems bent on revoking the rights of large swaths of the US population, I think a lot about the struggles that bind and implicate us. Already we are being deported, disappeared, incarcerated and erased. Hate is no "spooky" relationship. It is often very clear and estranging, a blade and gun. It causes despots to rise and bombs to fall.

*

"No one way works," Diana DiPrima writes, "it will take all of us shoving at the thing from all sides to bring it down."

*

Atlanta police and Georgia State troopers razed tents and arrested 28 student and faculty protestors at Emory University in April 2024. As at many other universities, Emory's administration created new rules limiting protest and prohibiting encampments. And yet, Emory students gathered for a pro-Palestinian demonstration as recently as September 2024.

EMORY IS EVERYWHERE.
THE PLACE FOR DIVISION IS NOWHERE.
WE INVITE YOU TO STRUGGLE WITH US.

The Israeli government's assault on Gaza continues with the Palestine Health Ministry estimating more than 54,000 Palestinians killed as of May 2025 at least half of whom were women and children.

Physicists tell us that "spooky" actions or "quantum entanglements" exist between particles such that "aspects of one particle of an entangled pair depend on aspects of the other particle, no matter how far apart they are or what lies between them," according to physicist Andreas Muller. These entanglements suggest that "when you measure something about one particle in an entangled pair, you immediately know something about the other particle, even if they are millions of light years apart." This relationship has been proven by strings of equations and decades of experiments; yet there remains no simple explanation for it. It exists beyond our laws or comprehension.

I find comfort that there is so much we still do not know about our universe or the rules that govern it or each other. I find comfort that we still can't predict what will happen when a young Palestinian uploads a video in Gaza or a college student in Georgia picks up a pen, when a Black sharecropper and organizer speaks to a predominantly white audience, or rallies white college students to register Black voters in Mississippi. It is impossible to know what relationships formed in protest and solidarity might produce in terms of new routes of exchange and support, new alliances and solutions.

*

In 1971, Hamer ended her speech in Madison, an off-the cuff performance ("I'm just here to rap and tell you what it is and to tell you like it is"), recounting a time just released from prison (where she was beaten until her "body was hard as metal") when she asked to be taken to see the Statue of Liberty:

> I told the man that I was riding with that day, I said, "I would like to see this statue turned around to face her own problems. And the torch out of her hand with her head bowed because we have as many problems in this country as they trying to point to in other countries."

I like to imagine the statue as Hamer wanted to see her: turning her head to look toward New Jersey and Manhattan, dropping her arm. If we could uncoil ourselves beyond the gestures of self-mythology and postures of our identities, if we could turn to face our own problems, what would we see?

There is nowhere "outside" of Emory University. Everywhere is Mississippi. It's 1964 and 2025. Our freedom is shackled to one another's. None of us are free until all of us are free to vote, to travel where we wish, to make choices about our own bodies. Free from bombs and hunger and brutality.

It is way past time we all drove down to Mississippi with our Wisconsin license plates. Get in the car.

POSTSCRIPT

If this book is a spreadsheet, it is also a spell, an incantation, a windshield flashing with sun. And rain. A document of grass crowding sidewalks, dropping flower and seed. Out of season like me. Russian thistle spun to tumbleweed, without our tending. It is also a book about poems as pockets of resistance: a taxi stalled at a rush hour intersection. (You be the white line, I'll be highway.) About our attempts to slip out from under the heel of capitalism. About a refusal to be complicit with the atrocities committed in the name of "citizenship," a burning tent, a library stormed by flame.

If this book is a check registry, it is also a love letter, an indictment. The memory of the woman, screaming *murderer, murderer, murderer*. On the G train. Another anthem. *Deny, Defend, Depose.*

I want whiteness to become as thin as a paycheck. I want capitalism to fray like the social safety net.

If this book is a series of monthly statements, it is also a ledger of questions:

Can we collaborate instead of nation? How do we "root" without becoming a gun in a glove box, an armored vehicle in the desert? How do we photosynthesize? Be a circle of soft green arrows on a classroom poster? (You be the watershed, I'll be the nimbus cloud.) How do we untangle the lyric from capitalism, from whiteness, from award season? How much would you give up because trying to hold on costs too much?

If this book is about money, it is also about the rupture, a rapture of rain in drought. About our attempts to remain in the wake of the category 5, the wildfire, the polar vortex. You should not need to be perfect to be safe. The money makes the weather. The wire transfers write history. The people who authorize our payments sift through the sky like an archive. The satellites ChatGPT us. The night learns to read our writing about the night.

I humbly submit to my board of directors (whomever you think you are) that my plan for growth is rebellion and rest/ riot, strike, riot/ improvise and nest. This book does not want to be a log of my productivity. *Was the investment worth the payout? Couldn't she have done more?* My genre is national hunger, economic trauma, debt.

I wrote some of these poems when the Dow Jones Industrial Average sank to 6,469, finished when it swelled to 42,570, and the Los Angeles wildfires raged, and a convicted rapist's election was certified. Defund, defend, develop for us.

This book is not inscribed onto bullets that kill CEOs, does not kill fascists, but wants to sing along with those who will sing the oligarchs to death. We refuse to be frayed as that social safety net. Let's poetry the tech bros. Lines breaking into shivs, the metaphors making tire irons. May we assemble like a sonnet, get projective in the streets, revise a history of soot into our seedling.

NOTES

"The Messengers" draws on the following source texts: "Comets Comets---an Introduction" from the European Space Agency website; "Heaven's Gate--How and When It May Be Entered" from the Heaven's Gate website; "How to Talk to the Dead" from WikiHow; Sabrina Imbler's "Developing Brains Fold Like Crumpled Paper to Get Their Convolutions," (*Scientific American*, 7 July 2015); Erin Kron's "Discourse with the Dead," (*Narratively*, 18 Oct 2013); Rebecca Morelle's "Near-death Experiences are Electrical Surge in Dying Brain" (BBC News, 13 Aug 2013) and Peter Sergo "Going Out with a Bang" (*Scientific American*, 1 April 2010).

In the poem **"Milkweed, Mirror, Windshield,"** the phrase "Not a mirror up to nature but —" comes from William Carlos Williams in *Spring and All*.

"The View from a Nation" contains an excerpt from a letter written by a migrant to the US President and given to the Kino Border Initiative for educational purposes. The excerpt is used here symbolically as a way to suggest an insistence that any consideration of the border must be founded upon the testimony of the people who have experienced forced migration, arrest, detention, and deportation.

In writing **"Toward the Shoreline"** I consulted the following sources: Reid Clement's *Submerged Forests*; Anne Carson's *Men in the Off Hours*; the *Investopedia* website; the video *Birth As We Know It*. (Dir. Elena Tonetti-Vladimirova); Christine Overall's *The New York Times* op-ed "Think Before You Breed" (17 June 2012); Julia Annas's *Plato: A Very Short Introduction*; David Benatar, *Better Never to Have Been: The Harm of Coming into Existence*; *The New York Times'* reporting on Hurricane Sandy; Richard Gray's article "Lost City of Heracleion Gives up Its Secrets" from *The Telegraph* (28 April 2013) and Yuheng Zhan's "Seriously Underwater" (*Business Insider*, 9 May 2024). For the purposes of this publication, I attempted to update some of the numbers in regard to economics. I avoided statistics shared from US government sources.

"Falls First" was written in response to artist Yuliya Lanina's painting of Vodianoy, a water spirit from a Russian folktale.

"My Documentarian" is for CD Wright.

"Up the Road:" I found then lost a newspaper photograph of my grandfather as a younger man than I ever knew him wearing suit and a large smile. My grandfather never went to school beyond eighth grade, worked as a gravedigger, a "loan collector," a boilerman. Despite his lack of formal education—or perhaps because of it—he read the newspaper every day. He joined a union. The share of US workers who belong to a union has fallen since 1983, when 20.1% of American workers were union members. In 2023, 10.0% of US workers were unionized. Views about the decline in union membership have changed only modestly since last year, when 58% said it was bad for the country. In journalism school, I was encouraged to write toward an audience at an eighth grade reading level, to write to my grandfather.

References to Charles Dickens' railroad accident in the poem **"Nail Guns in the Morning"** come from *The Railway Journey: The Industrialization of Time and Space in the 19th Century* by Wolfgang Schivelbusch. Nearly twenty years after its writing, the poem's final refrain remains sickeningly relevant.

"Chalk Marks on the Front Walk:" Both the calendula and the toddler were nurtured by Hoa Nguyen. So was I, so were my poems. I remain grateful to Hoa and to Dale Smith for their presence and friendship in Austin and in the years since.

"Isabella:" My father had the big shoulders of the white working class, of locks-the-doors and pays-the-bills. My father was safe as a government, came when you cried in the middle of the night. Except when he didn't. Except when he was away on business, except when he sprayed poison onthe lawn, when he smoked in the car while you slept in the backseat.

"Dear Mr. Director of the Census Bureau:" I sent copies of the poems that made up the original series to corresponding members of Pres. George W. Bush's administration (via snail mail). They never replied.

"Big Theory:" Power that doesn't look like power can crack concrete. My mother's worry could crumple freeways, could flatten the Polaski Skyway. My mother's worry could change the direction of a river. If by river you mean me. As if by mother, I could mean whiteness. I was a refugee from my mother's country. Power that doesn't look like power shapes lives. Pain radiates, a flock of birds twirling over our back yard, a murmuration of possibility. The rain freezing to puddle that cracks the concrete. That was my mother. Tree roots pushing up the sidewalk.

gone a little yellow like old teeth I have papaya I have tea last night was restless, a fight across the street, two shots fired I thought but it must have been the slam of the screen door. This morning I wake to another neighbor calling his dogs in from the driveway, nothing broke in the middle of the night. xx tree scarred and still growing anyway.

Slant rain coloring the screen, wind changing the rain, this morning this tree this demolition, construction something I built in sleep a small radio transistor, tight spiraled ceiling fan. Robert Moses drop the knife. the phone rings at 8:57óa little erasure, water on newsprint, checking off boxes or grading in a place ike a hotel with my father, the dream reminding me how much I missed my father as I answer the phone. The phone is a metaphor for that kind of communication, like the empty public bus is a metaphor for the dream sequence in the movie, when you are riding alone through Fort Green you must be dead or dreaming and the bus driver is black, and because he is your conduit he appears wise and will not speak to you. a view of religious suffering which links pain to sacrifice and sacrifice to exhaultation.

Rain now thick storm tussles trees, thick storm thrown across my front porch, tree roots knuckle the sidewalk.

"Alexander Litvinenko:" owes its title to the former Russian security agent turned dissident. As an exile living in London, Litvinenko authored several books critical of Russian President Vladmir Putin. He was murdered in 2006 by radioactive poisoning. Among the many wars that now rage unnamed, we fight now against people who rule the world like Putin or who want to rule the world like Putin without consequence, without end.

Other works that informed the poems in ***Utopia Minus*** include: *Photographic Views of Sherman's Campaign* (George Barnard), *Specimen Days* (Walt Whitman), *Travel Journals* (Herman Melville), *Geography of Nowhere* (James Howard Kunstler), *A Bibliography of America for Ed Dorn* (Charles Olson), *The New*

American Ghetto (Camilo José Vergara), *The Collected Writings* (Robert Smithson), an interview with Slavoj Žižek in support of Alfonso Cuarón's film *Children of Men*, *All That's Solid Melts Into Air* (Marshall Berman), and *The Shock Doctrine* (Naomi Klein).

The collage that forms the answer to the questions raised in the title of **"What does a Postmodern Poem Look Like?...."** includes excerpts from the following (clockwise from the top): Alice Notley's "Thinking and Poetry," Rachel Zucker's "Confessionalography: A GNAT (Grossly Non-Academic Talk) on 'I' in Poetry," bell hook's "Postmodern Blackness," CD Wright's "hills" and Juliana Spahr's "Introduction" to *American Women Poets in the 21st Century: Where Lyric Meets Language*. The questions on the following page are from Bhanu Kapil.

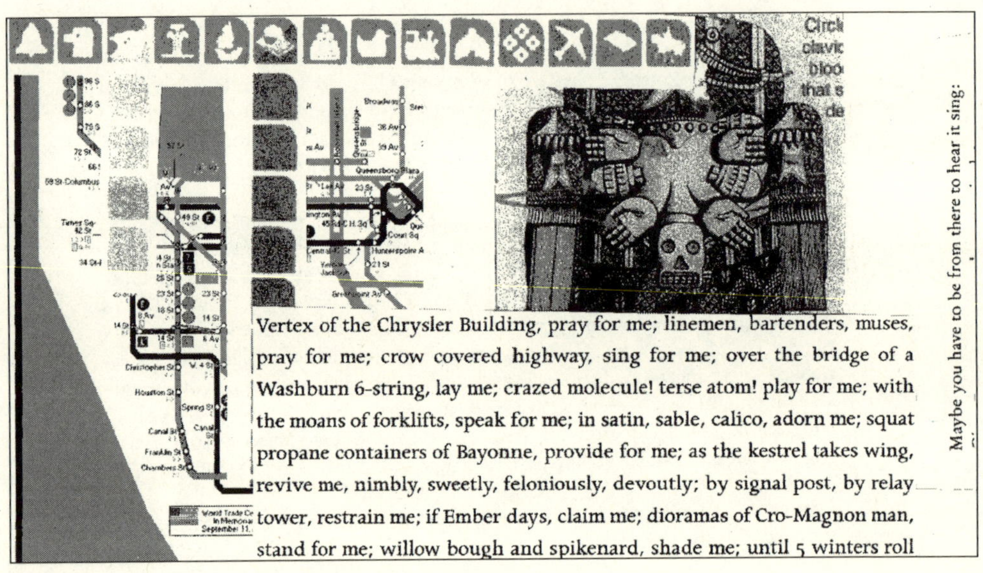

The collage for **"3rd Day of the Rainy Season"** includes excerpts from Roberto Tejada's poem "Amulet Anatomy" from *Full Foreground* as well as William Carlos Williams poem "The Ivy Crown" from *Journey to Love*. Certain lines in the "3rd Day Rainy Season" and other "Rainy Season" poems are lifted or paraphrased from *Psychoanalysis and Love* by André Tridon. The series is for Tejada and Rachel Levitsky.

"The Cartographer's Sons:" Else is the country you have yet to visit, the date on the calendar three pages or two clicks ahead. Else is next month's credit card bill, the statement that has not closed yet, the time you keep spending because you don't know what you can use to pay. Else is always a swipe away. Elsewhere, elsewhen, elsehow, elsewho.

The collage that forms the answer to the questions raised in the title of **"What does a Nonimperial Lyric Look Like?"** includes excerpts from Jorie Graham's poem "The Dream of the Unified Field," Bob Pearlman's "China," June Jordan's "Apologies to All the People in Lebanon" (with annotations by Eunsong Kim) and my essay "Seeing White" (Guernica Oct. 9, 2017). The question was inspired by Ariella Aïsha Azoulay's incitement to "unlearn imperialism." (See her book *Potential Histories Unlearning Imperialism*).

"Toward a Poetics of the Dow" takes some of its references from William Blake's "A Song of Liberty," Brenda Hillman's "A Violet in the Crúcible" (*Practical Water*), Lynn Hejinian's "The Rejection of Closure (1984)," John Lehrer's "A Physicist Solves the City" (*The New York Times Magazine* 17 Dec. 2010), Bernadette Mayer's *Midwinter Day* and Charles Olson's "A Later Note on Letter #15."

"October 14—The Dow Closes Up 10015" and other dated poems: For two years, I recorded the daily closing number of the Dow Jones Industrial Average. I plugged those numbers into various search engines (Project Gutenberg, Bartlett's quotations, and online versions of *Paradise Lost* and *Leaves of Grass*, to name a few). I allowed those texts to exert their influence over a series of poems—sometimes subtly, sometimes dramatically—in order to formally mimic the ways in which the closing number of the Dow exerts an influence over our lived experience. For example, **"October 14—The Dow Closes Up 10015"** found a seed in Ecclesiastes 1:18 (Bartlett's quotation 10015) and in a slippage between naming and knowing: "He that increaseth knowledge increaseth sorrow." As the project developed, I found other ways to let the closing number have an impact on the poem. Numbers continue to haunt: 70,000 tons of bombs dropped on Gaza in six months, the number of students arrested by police, amount of carbon in our atmosphere, miles of coral bleached. The air thickens with these numbers. "Number blindness" is the name for the condition by which we cannot conceive of any of it.

"November 25—The Dow Closes Up 10464" takes the phrase "When in doubt, win the trick," from *Twenty-four Rules for Learners* (Bartlett's quotation 10464). The line "Come out, come out, I am dying" comes from James Wright's poem "A Message Hidden in the Empty Wine Bottle That I Threw into a Gully of Maple Trees One Night at an Indecent Hour."

"December 7—The Dow Closes Up 10390" took inspiration from the phrase "spirit and matter" from the title of the first chapter *The Edinburg Lectures on Mental Science* by T. Trower (Project Guttenberg eText 10390).

The couplets reproduced here as the poems under the title **"Ticker"** ran along the bottoms of the pages in the original book mimicking a stock market ticker like the kind that frames our newsfeeds. The italicized sections come from Revelations, Michel de Certeau's *The Practice of Everyday Life* and *The Assets and Opportunity Score Card* (2012 by Jennifer Brooks and Kasey Wiedrich).

For the poems in the book's section **"The Market is a Parasite that Looks like a Nest"** I created a full-blown character to lay bare the market's personification. I imagined him white without thinking much about it. Which is whiteness: white behind the words, white hush, white noise. The Market blended into the sky it had bleached, faded into hospital corridors, into school hallways. The myth of white supremacy and capitalism. Horse and carriage, running off the road.

"May 14—The Dow Closes Down 10620" refers to the quotation: "The iron tongue of midnight hath told twelve" from *A Midsummer Night's Dream*. Act v. Sc. 1 (Bartlett's Quotation 620.)

In **"June 14—The Dow Closes Down 10192,"** the phrase "at first seems like a Graph Theory problem, but it is actually a simple Longest Common Subsequence (Dynamic Programming) problem" comes from entry UVa 10192 on the www.algorithmist.com wiki.

"October 29—The Dow Closes Down 11118" takes inspiration from Rilke's "Spanish Trilogy" instead of the market.

"The Market as Composition" takes the line "Nothing changes from generation to generation except the thing seen" from Gertrude Stein's "Composition as Explanation."

"Mother is Marxist" draws on the following source texts: US Census Bureau's per pupil expenditure reports, Spencer Ackerman's "41 men targeted but 1,147 people killed: US drone strikes–the facts on the ground," (*The Guardian*, 24 November 2014); Jo Becker's "Child Laborers in America in 2014," (Human Rights Watch, 17 Sept. 2014); Lewis Hines' photographs and documents from the National Child Labor Committee's Collection; Jaeah Lee's "Exactly How Often Do Police Shoot Unarmed Black Men?" (*Mother Jones*. 15 Aug. 2014); Andrew Schulz and G. W. Becker's "Local Cops Ready for War With Homeland Security-Funded Military Weapons," (*The Daily Beast. Newsweek/Daily Beast*, 21 Dec. 2011) and Viviana Zelizer's "The Price and Value of Children: the Case of Children's Insurance." (*American Journal of Sociology* 1981). The poem originally included a list of dates on which police killed unnamed African American women and men (Rich Juzwiak and Aleksander Chan's "Unarmed People of Color Killed by Police, 1999-2014." (*Gawker*, 8 Dec. 2014).

The collage that answers the question **"What does an Anticapitalist poem look like?"** includes a quote from Layli Long Soldier's poem "38" from her book *Whereas*.

In 2017 when I began writing ***Defacing the Monument***, information about obtaining asylum could be found on the US Department of Homeland Security's webpage entitled "Obtaining Asylum in the United States." When I concluded that book in 2019, the page simply entitled "Asylum," still did not mention the word "economic." There was, however, an alert on the top of the page referring to a recent US Citizenship and Immigration Services memorandum on procedures for "Unaccompanied Alien Children" that had been temporarily enjoined by court order.

As I write this in spring 2025, Amnesty International reports "the right to seek asylum in the United States is non-existent at the US-Mexico border, in violation of US human rights national and international obligations." Anyone apprehended by Immigration and Custom Agents face the prospect of detention and deportation. The Tr*mp administration has sent more than 200 to El Salvador's notorious Terrorist Confinement Center (CeCOT). A recent article in the *New Yorker* described them as "ghosts" in the US justice system.

Many factors contribute to the need to seek asylum. Both economic conditions and violence in Mexico and Central America (as well as in many other places around the globe) can be traced to decades of US policies. Among many sources see: Sayak Valencia's *Gore Capitalism* or Eduardo Galeano's *Century of the Wind*. Climate change has worsened many of these factors. For example, reporter Ryan Devereaux notes that in 2016: "the Food and Agriculture Organization of the United Nations reported that drought in Central America's dry corridor had left 3.5 million people in need of humanitarian assistance. USAID called it 'one of the worst droughts in 35 years in Central America.'" See Devereaux's "Mining the Future. Climate Change, Migration, and Militarization in Arizona's Borderlands," *The Intercept*, (3 Oct 2019).

Immigration policies have changed rapidly (and recklessly) during both of Tr*mp's and Biden's administrations. The information in these pages represents the policies and realities that were in place or unfolding at the time of its writing.

In **"No Where is Outside of Mississippi,"** quotes from Fannie Lou Hamer's University of Wisconsin speech come from *Speeches of Fannie Lou Hamer: To Tell It Like It Is* (University Press of Mississippi, 2011). My understanding of spooky attraction comes from Andreas Muller's article "What is quantum entanglement?" (*Astronomy*, 7, October 2020). Throughout this piece, I use the word "we" intentionally in solidarity, in the gesture of a large billowy tent, with the understanding that the tent doesn't cover all of us equality or some of us at all.

In the service of aesthetics, I ignored the chronological order of publication when arranging the works in this book.

BANKS GOT
BAILED OUT
GOT
Financial
Stock markets slide amid
warnings of a catastrophe
for the global economy
Stocks plunge in panic

ACKNOWLEDGMENTS

Grateful acknowledgment goes out to all the editors who published this work over the years. A special shoutout to the editors of the following journals (some of which are no longer publishing) and anthologies where the new work appeared, sometimes in an earlier version:

The Academy of American Poets Poem-a-Day, *Resist Much Obey Little* (anthology), *The Literary Review, Black Warrior Review, Stolen Island Poetry Review, Synecdoche, Bombay Gin, Essay Daily, Everyday Genius, The Virginia Quarterly Review, Imagined Theaters,* ecterapoetry.com, *Poems for Political Disaster* (*The Boston Review*), *A Dozen Nothing, Tupelo Quarterly*, and *Gulf Coast*

Thanks to VCCA's Moulin-A-Nef residency for the time and space and beauty to fuel this work.

Gratitude to all the those who worked on Ahsahta Press (the New Series) that published from 1999-2020.

Special thanks to Carmen Giménez, who published *Defacing the Monument* with Noemi Press, and to Mariah Bosch, Roda Avelar, Anthony Cody, Suzi F. Garcia, Sarah Gzemski and the rest of the team at Noemi.

Support small presses!

This was never my book alone: it is compilation of observations, reflections, recordings, and circumstance. A card of a book pulled from a deck of possibility. A book of collisions and relations, an arithmetic of anxiety and hope. A book of coincidences, of conversations.

To companions on the page and in IRL: Roberto Tejada, Dale Smith, Hoa Nguyen, Jenny Browne, CD Wright, Forrest Gander, Cecilia Vicuña, Divya Victor, Jen Scappetone, Juliana Spahr, Daniel Borzutzky, Giancarlo Huapaya, Rachel Galvin, Rosa Alcalá, Soham Patel, Lisa Robertson, Sarah Vap, Todd Fredson, Sara Sams, Bojan Louis, Roque Salas Rívera, Justin Petropolos, Rachel Levitsky, Ruth Ellen Kocher, Alan Michael Parker, Brenda Hillman, Bob Hass, Stephanie Pearmain, J. Michael Martínez, Bruce Smith, Campbell McGrath, Jane Miller, Valyntina Grenier, Julie Carr, Tonya Foster, Sam Ace, TC Tolbert, Claudia Rankine, Diana Delgado, David Taylor, Francisco Cantú, Anita Huízar Hernández, Sandy Soto, Nicole Antebi, Lee Anne Gallaway-Mitchell, Mónica de la Torre, Ander Monson, Taneum Bambrick, Sophia Terazawa, Claire Hong, Raquel Gutiérrez, James Hannaham, Brandon Shimoda, Dot Devota, Bhanu Kapil, Eileen Myles… I know this list is not complete….Thank you for your words, our correspondence and conversations, your example.

I love you!

To Gianna and Farid

endless love
our family is my favorite
ongoing creative collaboration

At least 50 percent of the royalties from this book will be donated to:

The Florence Immigrant and Refugee Rights Project
Mariposas Sin Fronteras

Please consider supporting these organizations!

To all of those who have made my food or coffee, cleaned the rooms where I taught and worked and wrote, for those who helped me care for my daughter for those who wrote grants for the presses and journals who published my work who printed + boxed + distributed + shipped the books, journals + anthologies I wrote (or wrote for) or read, to those who read or raised readers, to those who organized, protested, demanded + dreamed something better, to those who form the network that makes the best of this world and hopefully the next

This book is for you!

THE WORK NOT REGISTERED ON ANY TIMESHEET, NOT VALUED ON ANY STOCK INDEX

The poem is always and ever in dialogue with a thousand interlocutors, events, and sites of inspiration. Continue the conversation. Use these questions and prompts to write with me here.

How does a poem invite, transcribe or reflect a dialogue? How is your writing a social space? Diagram the voices and influences upon a single text you've written.

Conjure up the image of something you watched fall. Make a list of at least 10 words related to this falling. Write a poem from those words. Write another poem that resurrects the fallen.

Do you want a reminder of what was once stood, or do you want to redact it? Sketch your reminder or your redaction. Use words from your list above or the spaces they leave behind once you have erased them.

Record your thoughts and observations for the day. Record the closing number of the Dow Jones Industrial Average, the S&P 500, or the NASDAQ. Place that number into an online search engine Google or an online edition of Bartletts Famous Quotations or *Paradise Lost*. Allow that number to direct you to a text that you then allow to influence the poem you make from your thoughts and observations for the day. Observational and procedural, intimate and marked by the numbers that haunt our lives, like the hand of some unseen god.

When I shared *The Market Wonders* project with the poet Hayan Charara, we talked about his poem "The Prize" which begins with the lines:

> A book with poems
> about Bessie Smith,
> Marilyn Monroe,
> Queen Elizabeth,
> William Tell,
> W.B. Yeats,
> Ted Hughes,
> Sitting Bull,
> an otter, a fox, and a hare
> won the Pulitzer Prize
> in the first year
> of the war.

What other catalogs can you create? Investigate, then aspire reveal other legacies, histories, and synchronicities through your poem.

THE ONLY WAR THAT MATTERS IS THE WAR AGAINST THE IMAGINATION

...writes Diana Di Prima in "Rant" from *Revolutionary Letters* (a guidebook for this moment and the next.) Start imagining. Start investigating. Start spinning wishes and spells. Craft a detailed plan for breaking ICE arrestees out of detention centers. Imagine what a world without borders would look like. Craft a spell of self-protection for femme, trans and nonbinary people. Craft a plan of defense for femme, trans and nonbinary people. Share a remedy or cure. Let your poems function as plans and tools. If you can't write, draw, collage. Sometimes the image comes before the words. Know that you are creating an archive for the future.

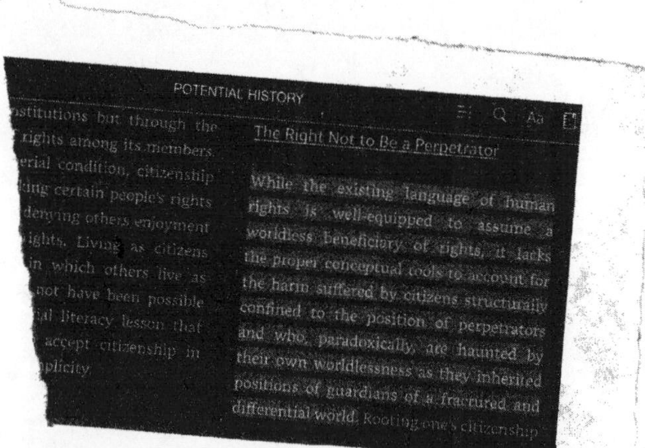

POTENTIAL HISTORY

nstitutions but through the
rights among its members.
erial condition, citizenship
king certain people's rights
denying others enjoyment
ights. Living as citizens
in which others live as
not have been possible
ial literacy lesson that
accept citizenship in
plicity.

The Right Not to Be a Perpetrator

While the existing language of human rights is well-equipped to assume a worldless beneficiary of rights, it lacks the proper conceptual tools to account for the harm suffered by citizens structurally confined to the position of perpetrators and who, paradoxically, are haunted by their own worldlessness as they inherited positions of guardians of a fractured and differential world. Rooting one's citizenship

from Ariella Aïsha Azoulay's Potential Histories